D1665695

SCHLEBRÜGGE.EDITOR

NATURE'S REVENGE

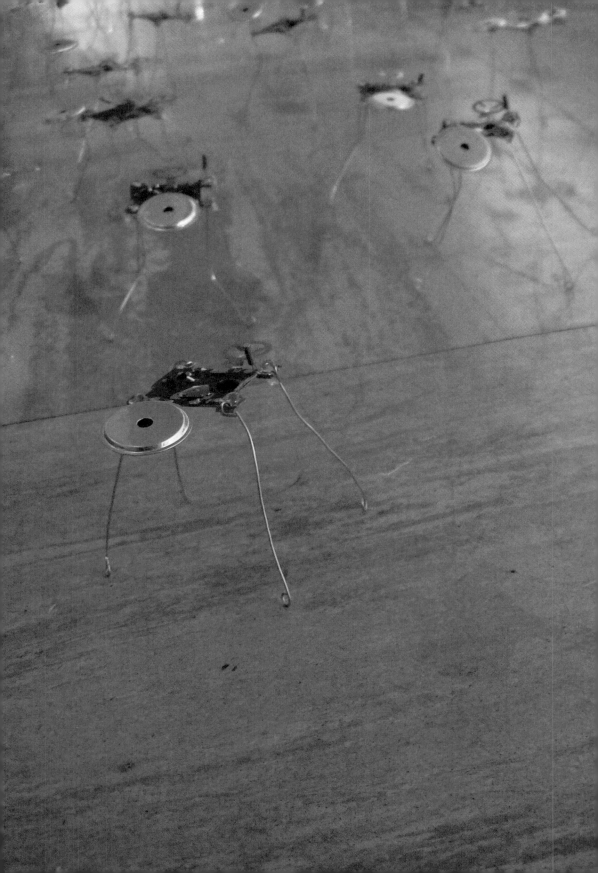

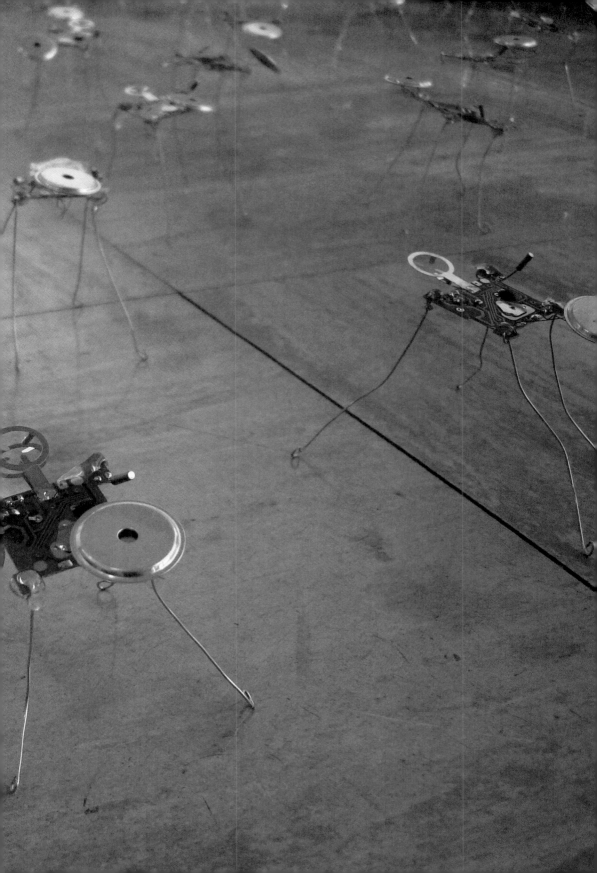

Inhalt | Contents

		S. | p.
Inhalt | Contents		11
Vorwort | Preface		12
Dandelion		14–21
Landcruiser		22–25
Kryptogamen | Cryptogamia		26–35
Thomas Feuerstein, Roland Maurmair	**Über die Kultur der Kryptogamen**	36–37
	On the Culture of Cryptogamia	38–39
and now something totally different		42–71
Bernhard Tilg	**n+1 Gorillas**	72–75
Tierversuche | Bioassays		78–80
Attacke! | Attack!		86–97
Die Afrikaner kommen! | The Africans are coming!		98–105
DoT – Depth of Texture		106–113
Sind wir nicht alle ein bisschen endo? | Aren't we all a little bit endo?		114–115
Otto E. Rössler	**Wir haben alles unter Kontrolle**	118
	Everything is under Control	121
Manfred Faßler	**Rabbitism**	122–127
Ein Häuschen im Grauen | A country cottage surrounded by grey shadows		128–133
Invasion of the Cyber Crickets		134–139
Tereza Kotyk	**Subversive Codes**	142–154
Pinocchio on World Tour		158–185
Herde – Rudel – Schwarm | Herds – Packs – Flocks		186–195
Inge Hinterwaldner	**Audiovisuelle Spannungen**	196–203
	Audiovisual tensions	204–208
houseberge		210–213
my home is my mountain		214–215
Elsbeth Wallnöfer	**mons ex machina**	216–227
Biographie | Biography		228
Werkverzeichnis | Index		230–233
Impressum | Colophon		235

Vorwort | Preface

Roland Maurmair

Schön, dass Sie vorbeischauen!
Zu sehen gibt's, neben Graphik und Installation, einen Tanz neuer Medien mit alten Technologien. Die Idee bestimmt das Format, dementsprechend vielfältig präsentiert sich meine Arbeit.

Es ist *Nature's Revenge*, wenn Neues über Altem wächst, aus Plastik ein neuer Urwald entsteht. Unser Abfall ist der Humus, auf dem zukünftige Generationen ihre Wirklichkeit erbauen.

An dieser Stelle ein großes Dankeschön an *Big Mama Nature* für all ihren Input.
Darüber hinaus bedanke ich mich bei den AutorInnen für ihre Unterstützung und bei all jenen, die mich über die Jahre getragen, begleitet und unterstützt haben.

Thanks for stopping by!
Apart from graphics and installations, this catalogue presents you with a dance of new media combined with old technologies. It is the idea that determines the format, which is reflected by the wide diversity of my work.

It is *Nature's Revenge* when new things grow on old remnants, and plastic is the soil for a new jungle. Our waste is the humus that future generations will build their reality on.

In this context, I would like to thank *Big Mama Nature* for all her input. In addition, many thanks for their help go to the authors contributing to this catalogue and all those who have accompanied and supported me over the years.

Morgen wird gestorben.

Dandelion

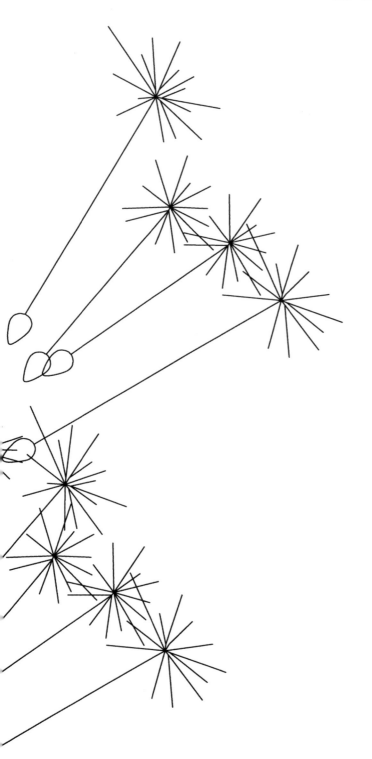

Dandelion

Klanginstallation 2006

Dandelion (dt.: Löwenzahn) ist einer Pusteblume nachempfunden.
Die Assoziation entsteht sowohl über den Titel der Arbeit wie auch durch die optische Erscheinung der Skulptur, welche im Zentrum des Raumes steht.

Windgeräusche und menschlich erzeugte Sounds sind der akustische Output der mit mit 64 Mini-Audioboxen bestückten Skulptur. Während das gezischte „Pst!" den Anwesenden zur Ruhe mahnt, dient das schnell und stichelnd hingeworfene „Ps, Ps" eher einem Anlocken. Durch veränderte Intonation, Lautstärke und die Möglichkeit, den Ton rund ums Objekt wandern zu lassen, ergeben sich mehrere Relationsoptionen zwischen dem Publikum und dem Kunstwerk und, auch wenn hier nur unilateral gesendet wird, verschiedene Variationen der Kommunikation.

Spricht man von Dolby Surround Systemen, meint man in der Regel, dass der Rezipient durch eine bestimmte Verteilung von Lautsprechern im Raum von Sound umgeben wird – *Dandelion* kehrt dieses Prinzip um: Im Zentrum steht die Skulptur und Klangquelle, umgeben von Zuhörern. Durch Differenzen und Überlagerungen entsteht, trotz des eindeutig bestimmbaren Klangzentrums, eine Entlokalisierung des Tons. Bewegt sich der Rezipient im Raum, verändert sich auch die akustische Erfahrung.

Analog zum biologischen Vorbild, bei dem der Wind die Samen fortträgt, mit der Bestimmung, dass diese auf fruchtbaren Boden fallen und den Fortbestand der Gattung sichern, verwickelt der akustische Sender bei dieser Installation den menschlichen Empfänger in eine Art Wechselspiel, auf dass das eine oder andere Wort im Ohr des Zuhörers seinen „rechten Platz" finden möge.

Eisenkonstruktion, 64 Audioboxen, Interface, PC

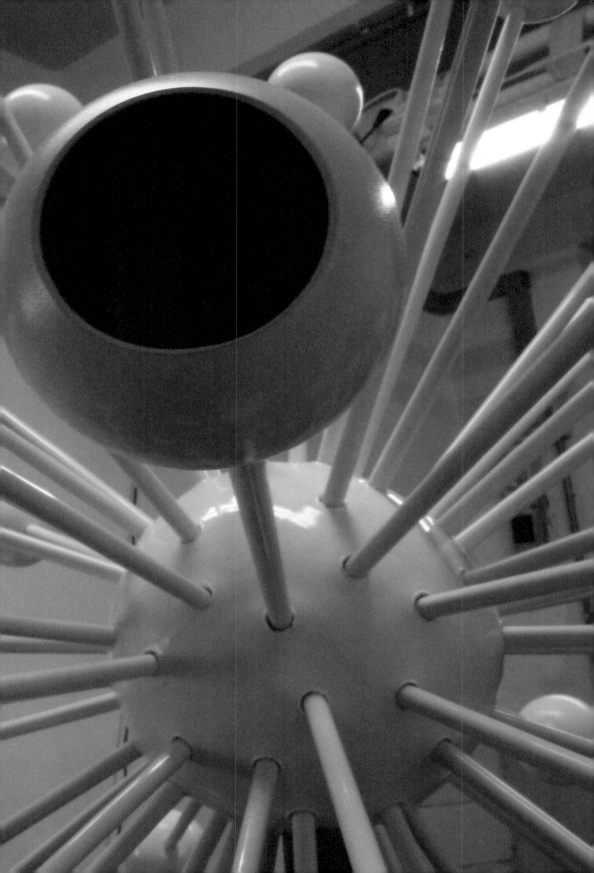

Dandelion

sound installation 2006

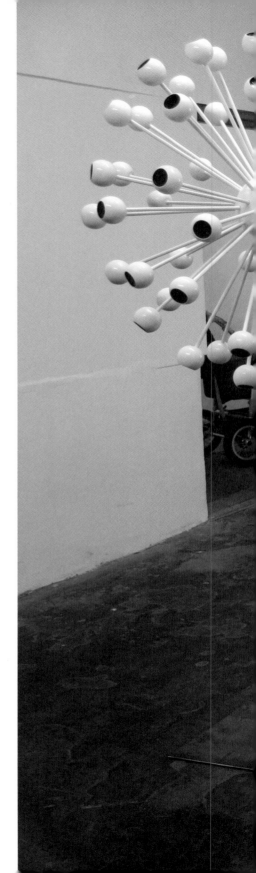

Dandelion is modelled on a blowball. The association is evoked by its title as well as the design of the sculpture, which features 64 mini audio boxes and is placed at the centre of the room.

The acoustic output consists of the sound of wind and man-made sounds. While a shushing sound reminds the audience to keep quiet, a rapid and challenging "ps, ps" is meant to encourage visitors to step closer. Changing intonation and volume as well as the possibility to let the sound travel around the object result in several opportunities for interaction between the audience and the piece of art, and various possible ways of communication even though the sound is emitted in one direction only.

A dolby surround system usually enables the listener to be surrounded by sound due to a certain distribution of loudspeakers around the room. *Dandelion* is a reversal of this principle: It is the sculpture and sound source that are at the centre surrounded by the audience. Differences and interferences lead to a delocalisation of the sound despite the clearly identifiable centre of the sound. Each movement that the recipient makes across the room changes his acoustic experience.

Similar to its biological role model, where the wind carries away the seed so that they may fall on fertile ground and ensure the survival of the species, the acoustic transmitter in this installation creates some kind of interaction with the human recipient, hoping that one word or another may find their "right place" in the listener's ear.

Iron construction, 64 audio boxes, interface, PC

Landcruiser

Landcruiser

Interaktive Rauminstallation 2002/03

Fällt ein Stein auf die Erde, auch wenn niemand es bemerkt? Treffender formuliert: Existiert man eigentlich auch dann, wenn niemand es sieht? Das alte Spiel zwischen Wahrnehmung und Wirklichkeit wird zur Groteske, denkt man nur an die unzähligen Kameras in Kaufhäusern, in Banken, in der U-Bahn, oder an die lückenlose Überwachung durch Satelliten im öffentlichen Raum. Mit dem Bewusstsein immer und überall beobachtet zu werden, immerzu medial präsent zu sein, entsteht eine starke Abweichung des Individualverhaltens in unserer Gesellschaft. Paranoid gemacht durch die Medien, kommuniziert der Mensch nicht mehr auf direktem Wege, sondern alles durchläuft zuvor eine Art Filter namens *Political Correctness*. Der Mensch schafft Realitäten, die wieder auf ihn zurückwirken und ihn beeinflussen. Anders gesagt befinden wir uns in einem rekursiven Akt, in dem Form uns gleichermaßen bedingt wie wir die Form.

Aufbau:
Eine Modellwelt (überwuchert von organischem Material) bildet das Herzstück dieser Arbeit. Durch eine via Joystick gesteuerte Kamera erhält der Benützer die Möglichkeit, diese Modellwelt in einem Spektrum von 360 Grad zu "umfliegen". Die Projektion dieser satellitären Betrachtung erfolgt auf eine im Raum befindliche Fläche. Beim "Scannen" der Oberfläche des Globus trifft der Betrachter auf vorweg definierte Punkte, die als "Pforten" zu einer virtuellen Realität zu verstehen sind. Die Animationen, die an diesen spezifischen Punkten abgespielt werden, lassen den Betrachter in eine Welt eintauchen, die einen fließenden Übergang vom virtuellen zum realen Raum zulässt.

Eisenkonstruktion, Motoren, Kugel mit organischem Material, Kamera, Licht, Joystick, Interface, Pc

interactive multimedia installation 2002/03

Does a stone fall on the ground even when nobody sees it? In other words: Do we exist even when nobody sees it? The old game about perception and reality becomes grotesque considering the innumerable cameras in shopping malls, banks and the underground, or the constant and full satellite surveillance in the public sphere. Being aware of the fact that we are constantly surveyed whenever and wherever we go, i.e. permanently present via some kind of medium, individual behaviour has been subject to considerable deviations in our society. As the media have made us paranoid, we do not communicate directly any longer but apply a kind of filter called "political correctness" before any kind of communication can take place. Man creates realities, which in turn act and impact on him. In other words, we are part of a recursive function in which the curve determines us and we determine the curve.

Structure:
A model world (overgrown by organic material) is at the heart of this piece of work. With the help of a joystick controlling a camera, the user can fly around this model world within a 360-degree spectre. This satellite image seen through the camera is projected onto a screen in the room. When scanning the surface of the model world, the onlooker comes across spots previously defined by the artist as portals to a virtual reality. The short films the visitor can see when directing the camera towards these spots are the element in this piece of work that creates some kind of surreality through the gradual transition from virtual to real space.

Iron construction, engines, ball with organic material, camera, light, joystick, interface, PC

Kryptogamen

Die im Geheimen Hochzeit Haltenden

Kryptogamen, geheimblühende oder blütenlose Pflanzen, werden wissenschaftlich gesehen in 14 Klassen unterteilt. Bei meiner künstlerischen Auseinandersetzung habe ich mir eine Vorauswahl erlaubt und mich mit einzelnen Klassen intensiv beschäftigt. Die folgenden vier Arbeiten wurden für die Ausstellung „Die Ordnung der Natur" im OK-Centrum Linz adaptiert beziehungsweise neu realisiert.

Cryptogamia

marrying in hiding

Scientifically speaking cryptogamia, which are secretly-flowering or non-flowering plants, are classified into 14 categories. However, I have made a pre-selection and will deal with certain categories only. The following four pieces of work were adapted and readjusted for "The Order of Nature" exhibition at the OK Centre in Linz, Austria.

Algen.html

Siebdruck auf Nori-Algen 1998/2005

Html Source Code & ASCII-Code als direkte Analogie zur organischen Beschaffenheit von Algen.

```
TLE>cryptogamen.html</TITLE>
D>
ESET ROWS="*,400,*" FRAMEBORD
E SRC="algen.html" NAME="Top"
ESET COLS="*,500,*" FRAMEBORD
E SRC="algen.html" NAME="Left
ESET ROWS="100,280,40" FRAMEB
ESET COLS="100,420" FRAMEBORD
E SRC="logo.html" NAME="logo"
E SRC="logotext.html" NAME="l
MESET>
ESET COLS="100,400" FRAMEBORD
E SRC="main.html" NAME="colon
E SRC="output.html" NAME="out
MESET>

NAME="GENERATOR" CONTENT="nothing sp
E>algen.html</TITLE>
```

Algae.html

screen print on Nori algae 1998/2005

Html Source Code & ASCII code in direct analogy to the organic structure of algae.

moos

Installation 1998/2005

Ein Fernsehgerät zeigt, wie Wassertropfen senkrecht in Richtung einer Audiobox fallen. Zwischen diesen beiden ist das Wort *moos* aufgedruckt. Der „Aufprall" wird temporär verzögert, wodurch der Eindruck entsteht, dass die Tropfen die Materialität des Textes überwinden müssten.

moss

installation 1998/2005

On a TV screen the visitor can see water drops that are falling towards an audio box. The word *moss* is printed between them. There is a delay in time before the water drops "hit" the box, which leaves the visitor with the impression that the drops first have to overcome the materiality of the text.

moos

Farn

Installation 2004/2005

Diese Arbeit bezieht sich auf die Fortpflanzung, welche bei Farnen via Sporenabkapselung passiert, wobei hier keine biologische Abhandlung verbildlicht werden soll, sondern eine poetische Auseinandersetzung stattfindet.

Ein Video wird auf einen Regenmantel projiziert, jedoch nur unvollständig, da allein dessen bedruckte Stellen auch als Projektionsfläche taugen. Zusätzlich wird die Projektion von einem feinen Wasserschleier umhüllt, sodass immer nur flüchtige Fragmente des Gezeigten erhascht werden können.

Regenmantel & Plexiglasscheiben bedruckt, Wasserdampf, Videoprojektion, Koje

Fern

installation 2004/2005

Reproduction is the core theme of this work. Ferns reproduce via spores that are dispersed; however, this work is not intended to demonstrate a biological system but is an attempt to deal with the subject on a poetic level.

A video is projected onto a raincoat, but the projection is incomplete since only the printed parts can serve as a projection surface. Besides, the projection is covered by a thin layer of water so that you can only catch fleeting glimpses of is being shown.

raincoat & printed plexiglass, water steam, video projection, booth

Bärlappfeldgenerator

Interaktive Installation 2005

Eine vordefinierte Abfolge von Sinusfrequenzen versetzt eine Membran, auf welcher sich Bärlappsporen befinden, in Bewegung. Spricht oder singt man in ein für diesen Zweck beigestelltes Mikrofon, werden diese Frequenzen unterbrochen und die Bärlappsporen derart in Schwingung versetzt, dass sich unterschiedlichste Sprach-Muster bilden – es entsteht Lautmalerei im wortwörtlichen Sinn. Ganze Dialoge werden visualisiert und erzeugen immer neue Sprachbilder. Gleichzeitig mit der Erkenntnis über die Begrenztheit unserer Wahrnehmung werden wir an die Existenz morphischer Felder in unserer Umwelt erinnert, die wir mit den Sinnesorganen nicht wahrzunehmen vermögen – es entsteht sozusagen eine „Blindenschrift für Sehende". Das gesprochene Wort wird zur Aktion.

Bärlappsporen, Unterkonstruktion, Membran, Mikrophone, PC

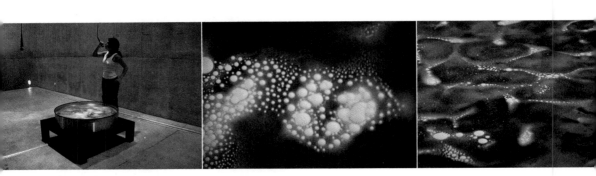

Club Moss Field Generator

interactive installation 2005

A pre-defined sequence of sinus frequencies sets into motion a membrane that is covered by club moss spores. As soon as someone starts to speak or sing into the microphone placed above it for this purpose, these frequencies are interrupted and the club moss spores start to vibrate so that a variety of different language patterns form – i.e. tone painting in its most literal sense. Entire dialogues are visualised, and new images constantly created. Realizing the limitations of our perception, we are reminded of the existence of morphogenetic fields in our surroundings that we cannot perceive with our sensory organs – a "Braille system for the non-blind" is created. The spoken word triggers action.

Club moss spores, subconstruction, membrane, microphones, PC

Über die Kultur der Kryptogamen

Aus einem Gespräch zwischen Roland Maurmair und Thomas Feuerstein

Aus menschlicher Perspektive sind Kryptogamen (blütenlose Pflanzen wie u.a. Algen, Moose, Flechten) Lebewesen, die man buchstäblich mit Füßen tritt. Sie spielen eine untergeordnete Rolle und bilden gleichsam den Bodensatz, über den man hinwegläuft. Kryptogamen sind bescheidene Pflanzen, die in der Ordnung der Natur zwar ganz unten stehen, mitunter die Ordnung der Kultur jedoch stören; etwa die heile Ordnung der Gartenmauer oder des Wochenendhauses. Als Pionier-pflanzen dringen sie meist unbemerkt überallhin vor und besiedeln als Kulturfolger Dachziegeln und Betonritzen. Sie stören und zerstören die zivilisatorische Ordnung von ästhetisch gereinigten und verkitschten Idyllen. In diesem Sinne verkörpern sie die biologische Information, welche die kulturelle mit Entropie bedroht. Und insofern haben diese Organismen aufgrund ihres entwick-lungsgeschichtlich hohen Alters nicht nur etwas Archaisches, sondern auch etwas Anarchisches, da sie Lebensräume zurückreklamieren.

Einerseits hat dies etwas Beruhigendes, Romantisches, andererseits aber auch etwas Bedrohliches, weil der Mensch angesichts dieser Pflanzen sich seiner eigenen Vergänglichkeit und der seiner Kultur bewusst wird. Diese Urpflanzen stehen am Anfang der Evolution und werden höchstwahr-scheinlich über die menschliche Kultur hinaus Bestand haben. Sie sind ein konstitutiver Bestandteil für das Leben auf unserem Planeten, weil sie am Beginn der „Ordnung der Natur" stehen. Aber gleichzeitig stehen sie für die Apokalypse dieser Ordnung, denn wenn alles wieder vergeht, sind sie jene Pflanzen, die am längsten auf unseren Gräbern ausharren werden. Kryptogamen sind nicht nur urgeschichtlich, sie sind vor allem zukunftsgeschichtlich. (...)

Interessant sind diese Pflanzen auch, da sie der Entwicklung müde zu sein scheinen, kaum mutie-ren und ihr Genom sich äußerst stabil verhält. Es handelt sich um Lebewesen, die sich der Evolution verweigern und dem Fortschrittsgedanken entziehen. Vergleichbar mit subversiven, atavistischen Primitiven demonstrieren sie über Low-Tech-Beharrlichkeit und setzen sich entschleunigend über die Zeit hinweg. Technisch betrachtet könnten sie als entwicklungsresistente, konservative Ver-weigerungspflanzen beschrieben werden, die in Bezug auf unsere neugierige und auf Fortschritt konzentrierte westliche Kultur antiavantgardistisch erscheinen. Vielleicht sind Kryptogamen die „Future Primitives" der Botanik. (...)

Die Kryptogamen (griech. die im Verborgenen heiraten) sind jene, die es sprichwörtlich im Gehei-men treiben. Uns Menschen ist dieses Verhalten, egal ob wir monogam oder polygam leben, ver-traut. Sexuell wären die Kryptogamen die Verschämten, politisch wären sie aber die im Geheimen operierenden Ungehorsamen und Gefährlichen, die Delinquenten, Gesetzlosen, Verschwörer oder Terroristen. Was im Geheimen passiert, unterläuft System und Apparat. Kryptogamen treiben keine öffentlichen Blüten, streben nicht nach Aufmerksamkeit, sondern huldigen der Absenz und dem Verschwinden. Sie entziehen sich der Wahrnehmung und Kontrolle, womit das Kryptogame nicht nur die Bedeutung des Verkappten und Verschämten hat, sondern gerade in einer mediatisierten und überwachten Gesellschaft auch den Aspekt des Kryptologischen beinhaltet. Der Wunsch oder die Notwendigkeit, sich einer technisch „aufgeklärten" und überwachten Gesellschaft zu entzie-hen, geht mit der Schaffung „kryptischer" Orte und Codes einher.

Eine andere geheimnisvolle Seite der Kryptogamen liegt im Phantastischen. Denkt man etwa an Algen, so sind Kryptogamen auch Pionierpflanzen menschlicher Phantasie. Sie tauchen in Science-Fiction-Literatur auf, sollen beim Terraforming fremder Planeten helfen, werden von der NASA als Proteinquelle für Astronauten in Betracht gezogen, sollen in Anti-Aging-Produkten die Jugend erhalten, in der Medizin Krebs bekämpfen, eine universelle Nahrungs- und Rohstoffquelle bilden und Erdöl genauso wie Rindfleisch ersetzen. Das Archaische und Futurologische verknüpft sich in den Kryptogamen auf wundersame Weise: Seit dem 19. Jahrhundert ist unsere Kultur von einer Nekrophilie toter Kryptogamen in Form von Kohle und seit dem 20. Jahrhundert in Form von Erdöl beherrscht. Das 21. Jahrhundert wird aber jenes sein, wo diese Nekrophilie der toten Pflanzen einer Biophilie der lebenden Pflanzen weichen wird. Kryptogamen wird es also nicht mehr nur fossil an der Tankstelle geben, sondern auch nachhaltig und frisch auf dem Teller, in der Creme, als Medikament, als Kunststoffersatz und vielleicht sogar als Informationsträger in Biorechnern.
Genau an diesen Punkten berührt das Primitive High-Tech-Kategorien, wird das Atavistische futuristisch.

On the Culture of Cryptogamia

Roland Maurmair in conversation with Thomas Feuerstein

From the human perspective, cryptogamia (seedless plants such as algae, moss and lichens) are living creatures that we literally walk all over. They play a subordinate role and at the same time form the ground on which we stand. Cryptogamia are humble plants, which are very low-ranking in the order of nature, but nonetheless manage to disrupt the idyllic order imposed by culture, for example the sacrosanct order of the garden wall or weekend house. As pioneering vegetation, they make clandestine forays into their environs, settling on the heels of civilisation in roof tiles and cracks in the concrete. They disturb and destroy the civilized order of aesthetically scrubbed and kitschified idyllic landscapes. In this sense, they embody the biological information that threatens to condemn cultural achievements to entropy. As some of the oldest forms of life on the planet, they have not only an archaic quality, but also a touch of anarchy, a way of barging in to reclaim habitats and return them to their original state.

There is something reassuring and romantic about this, but also an undertone of menace, a reminder of the ultimate transience of humankind and its culture. These primeval plants already proliferated on earth in the early days of evolution, and will in all probability outlast human civilisation. They are the constituent component of life on our planet, because they form the very beginning of the „order of nature". But at the same time they also stand for the apocalypse of this order: when everything else is dead and gone, these are the plants that will survive the longest on our graves. Cryptogamia are not only prehistoric, they are above all posthistoric. (...)

Another interesting aspect of these plants is that they seem to be tired of developing, hardly mutating at all any more and manifesting a genome that is exceptionally stable. These living creatures refuse to cooperate with evolution and turn up their noses at the idea of progress. Like subversive, atavistic primitives, they demonstrate against the common trend with their low-tech perseverance and obdurate deceleration in apparent indifference to the march of time. In technical terms, they could be described as development-resistant, conservative, non-cooperative plant forms, taking an anti-avant-garde stance in opposition to our inquisitive and progress-enamored western culture. Perhaps cryptogamia are the „Future Primitives" of botany. (...)

Cryptogamia (Greek for „those who marry in secret") are literally those who mate in secret. We as humans are familiar with such behavior, whether monogamous or polygamous. Sexually, the cryptogamia would correspond with those who are bashful. Politically, though, they might be the covertly operating civil disobedients, the delinquents, the lawless, conspirators or terrorists. Whatever happens underground undermines the system and the regime. Cryptogamia do not produce any public flowers, do not try to attract attention, but instead pay homage to absence and disappearing. They elude perception and control, evoking associations with the hidden and coy, but also, in the context of a society heavily influenced by media and surveillance, taking on a cryptological aspect. The need or desire to escape from the clutches of a technologically „enlightened" and monitored society goes hand in hand with the creation of „cryptic" places and codes.

Another mysterious side of the cryptogamia is their fantasy factor. If one thinks of algae, for instance, it is evident that cryptogamia are also pioneering plants in the human imagination. They make frequent appearances in science fiction literature, are to be enlisted to help in terraforming alien planets, are under consideration by NASA as a potential protein source for astronauts, they are touted in anti-aging products for their rejuvenating properties, used in medicine to fight cancer, form a universal nutritional source and useful raw material, and can replace both petroleum and beef. The cryptogamia represent a fascinating fusion of the archaic and the futuristic. Since the 19th century, our culture has been ruled by necrophilia for dead cryptogamia in the form of coal and since the 20th century in the form of oil. But the 21st century will be the one in which this necrophilia for dead plants makes way for a biophilia of living ones. Cryptogamia will be available not ony in their fossilized form at the gas station, but also sustainable and fresh on our plates, in creams, as medicine, as plastic substitute and perhaps even as data carriers in bio-computers.

Here is where primitive comes into contact with high-tech, where atavistic becomes futuristic.

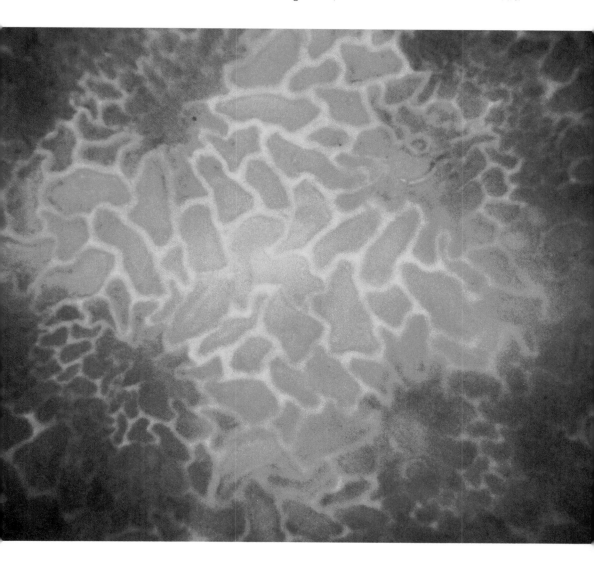

and now something

totally different...

go wild!

Statische Versuchsanordnung 1996

Tisch 1: Pulsierende Eisenpartikel als Analogie zur magnetischen Tonbandaufzeichnung.
Tisch 2: Plattennadel, die die Erschütterungen im Raum anolog überträgt und dadurch die Ordnung der Partikel verändert.

Eisenpulver, Lautsprecher, Plattennadel, Spule, Licht, Eisentische, Glas

---

static experimental design 1996

Table 1: Pulsating iron particles in analogy to the magnetic tape recording.
Table 2: Turntable needle analogously transmitting the vibrations in the room, thus changing the order of the particles.

iron powder, loudspeaker, turntable needle, spool, light, iron tables, glass

Auslage in Arbeit

Partizipatorische Installation 1999

Aquarium, Polarisationsfilter, Siebdruck mit Euglena Viridis

Work in progress

participatory installation 1999

aquarium, polarizing filter, screen print with Euglena Viridis

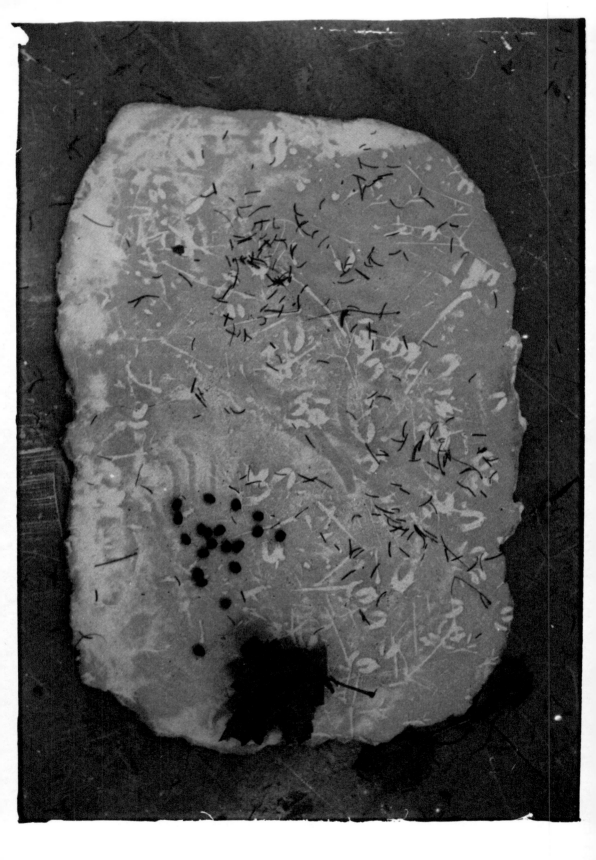

el viento viene, el hombre se va

Intermediale Installation 2000

Ein Ventilator bläst, im Fernseher bewegen sich Blätter im Wind. Am Boden befinden sich vier Tonplatten mit Abdrücken tierischer und menschlicher Spuren.

4 Tonplatten, TV, Video, Ventilator, Rehkot, Kaugummi, Blätter

---

media installation 2000

A fan is blowing, inside the TV leaves are moving in the wind. On the floor there are four clay plates with animal and human imprints.

4 clay plates, TV set, video, fan, deer faeces, chewing gum, leaves

kluft reloaded

Lichtobjekt 2004/2007

Holzkasten (100x20x21cm), Bergkristalle, Licht

Cleft reloaded

light object 2004/2007

wooden case (100x20x21cm), crystallized
quartz, light

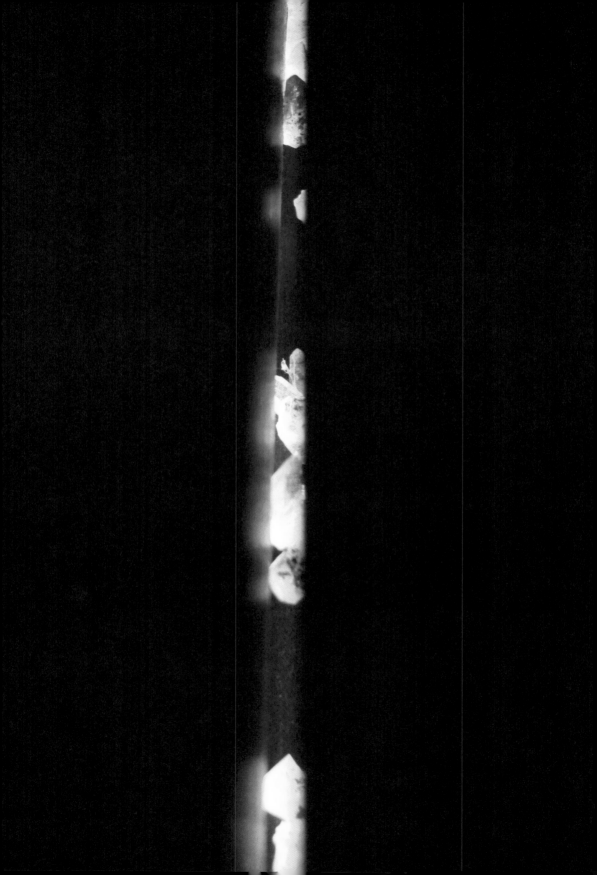

Kastanienaktion

Intervention 2003
Kastanien bemalt und wieder im öffentlichen Raum verteilt

Chestnut action

intervention 2003
painted chestnuts returned to the public space

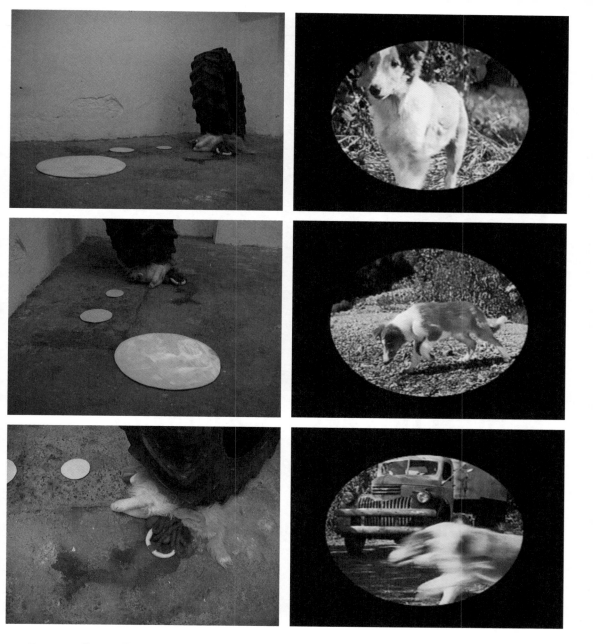

Lassies letzter Augenblick

Installation 2005
Traktorreifen, Stoffhund, Video-Projektion, Filz, Farbe

Lassie's last moments

installation 2005
tractor tyres, stuffed dog, video projection, felt, paint

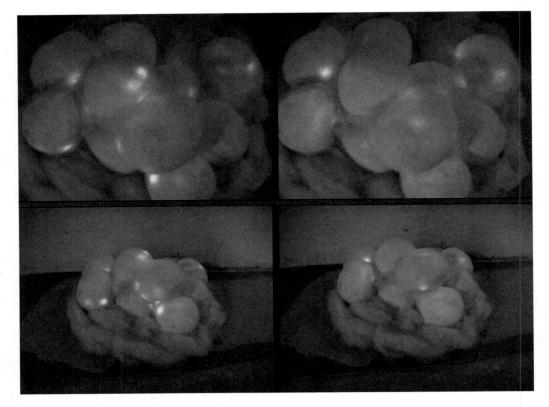

Mach das Licht aus, wenn Du gehst

Installation 2005/2008
Audiobox, CD-Player, Meeresrauschen, Teppich, Sand, Filzeier, Lichterkette, Schildkröte, Filz

---

Turn off the lights when you leave

Installation 2005/2008
audio box, CD player, murmur of the sea, carpet, sand, felt eggs, light chain, turtle, felt

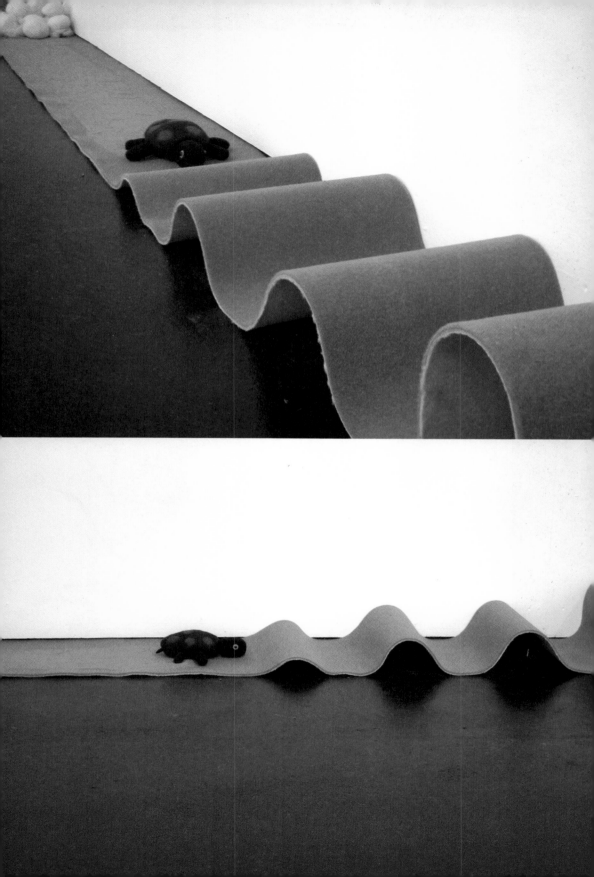

Schmos'ma? MALLNAIT 2009

These hips are made for shaking

Installation 2007
Kuhglocken, Gummibänder, Screen, DVD-Player, Video

---

installation 2007
Cow bells, elastic bands, screen, DVD player, video

Blinde Kuh

links: Zeichnung 2005 | rechts: Performance 2008

Blind man's buff

left: drawing 2005 | right: performance 2008

Punkcorn

Punkcorn

Lichtinstallation 2008

Ein Motor im Inneren bewegt die Alufolie, sodass ein Knistern zu hören ist, ähnlich wie bei der Zubereitung von Popcorn.

Alufolie, Motor, Seile, Halogenspots

---

light installation 2008

An engine at the centre of the installation keeps the aluminium foil in motion, making it sound somewhat like bursting pop corn.

aluminium foil, engine, ropes, halogen spotlights

Porno

Radierung, Installation | etching, installation 2008

Gefahrenquelle

Intervention 2011

Stoffbanane, Bananenschalen, Schilder

Source of Danger

intervention 2011

fabric banana, banana peels, signs

n+1 Gorillas

Art, space and theory

Bernhard Tilg

Gorillas am Fenster und im Fernsehen. Multitude, Horde, Tribes, Migrationsgruppen, Urban Development und kleine Vogelnester. Objekte, Grafiken, Videos, intermediale Installationen und statische Versuchsanordnungen – immer bewegt sich Roland Maurmair an den Schnittstellen der diskursiven Disziplinen, das Experiment ist dabei eine zentrale Methode seiner Arbeitsweisen.

Wenn Lyotard die Aufgabe eines Philosophen oder Künstlers darin sieht, die Regeln des eigenen Tuns zu reflektieren und zu erweitern, so erfüllt Maurmair diese Aufgabe inhaltlich wie formal voll und ganz. Die kategoriale Trennung von Wissenschaft und Kunst wird kategorisch zurückgewiesen, insofern – wie Deleuze und Guattari sagen – alles gleichzeitig berücksichtigt werden muss, und es notwendig wird, dass die Künstler/innen selbst zu Theoretikern/innen und Philosophen/innen werden. Zugleich werden aber die Theoretiker/innen und Philosophen/innen auch Künstler/innen, und schaffen „Theorie-Fiktionen" zur Herstellung von Mikrologien und Mikro-Universen und um die Frage nach den Bedingungen und den Möglichkeiten dieser Prozesse stellen zu können. Insofern stellt Lyotard folgerichtig fest: „Alles [...] bei Duchamp ist Forschungsarbeit, reine Forschung."[1] Maurmairs Werke sind, von dieser Warte aus gesehen, Forschungsergebnisse einer intersubjektiven und transdisziplinären Arbeit.

„Dadurch wird die Unterscheidung zwischen Wissenschaft und Kunst hinfällig werden: die Wissenschaft wird als eine intersubjektive Fiktion, die Kunst als eine intersubjektive Disziplin zwecks Erkenntnissuche erscheinen, also die Wissenschaft als eine Kunstart, und die Kunst als eine Variante der Wissenschaft."[2]

Dabei geht es auch um die Frage, warum die Kunst in unserer Gesellschaft nur eine Beziehung zu den Gegenständen, nicht aber zum Leben und dem Individuum unterhält. Daraus ergibt sich auch ein Unbehagen an der (gegenwärtigen) Kultur, welches Maurmair immer wieder artikuliert und thematisiert: Die fehlende Beziehung zu uns selbst als Subjekt und Objekt in der Weise, als das unsere je eigene Existenz zwar als Ergebnis diskursiver Praktiken verstanden werden muss, zugleich aber unsere Existenz ihrerseits, als Material der Sorge, der Veränderung und des Werdens, nicht mehr in der Lage ist, ästhetische und ethische Existenzweisen zu begründen. „Kunst und Wissenschaft werden dann als ‚politische Disziplinen' angesehen werden müssen."[3]

---

1   Lyotard, Jean-François: Philosophie und Malerei im Zeitalter ihres Experimentierens, Berlin 1986, S.37
2   Flusser, Vilém, in: Philosophie der neuen Technologien, Berlin 1989, S.54
3   Flusser, Vilém, in: Philosophie der neuen Technologien, Berlin 1989, S.54

n+1 Gorillas

Art, space and theory

Bernhard Tilg

Gorillas at the window and on TV. Multitudes, hordes, tribes, migration groups, urban development and little bird nests. Objects, graphics, videos, inter-media installations and statistical test assemblies – Roland Maurmair keeps moving along the interfaces of discursive disciplines, experiments forming a central method of his techniques.

If Lyotard deems that it is the philosopher's or artist's job to reflect and extend the rules of his own behaviour, Maurmair fully accomplishes this task both on the content and on the formal level. The categorical separation of the arts and sciences is rejected categorically since – as postulated by Deleuze and Guattari – everything needs to be considered, and artists themselves are now required to become theoreticians and philosophers. But theoreticians and philosophers are equally turning into artists, creating theoretical fiction in order to produce micrologies and micro-universes and raise questions about the conditions and possibilities of these processes. In this context, Lyotard correctly states, "With Duchamp […] everything is research, nothing but research."[1] From this point of view, Maurmair's works are the result of inter-subjective and trans-disciplinary research.

"Thus, it will no longer be necessary to distinguish between science and art: Science will turn into inter-subjective fiction, art will turn into an inter-subjective discipline aimed at finding answers; in other words, science will become art, and art will become a form of science."[2]

Another issue that is addressed in this context is the question of why art in our society only relates to objects rather than life and the individual. It also creates an uneasy feeling towards (today's) culture, which has repeatedly been articulated and addressed by Maurmair. The missing relationship to ourselves as objects and subjects, in such a way that our own existence must be considered the result of discursive practices, while our existence, the very material of sorrow, change and transition, is not capable any longer of founding aesthetic and ethic ways of existence. "The arts and science will then have to be regarded as political disciplines."[3]

1   Lyotard, Jean-François: Philosophy and Painting in the Experimental Age, Berlin 1986, p.37
2   Flusser, Vilém, in: Philosophy of the new Technologies, Berlin 1989, p.54
3   Flusser, Vilém, in: Philosophy of the new Technologies, Berlin 1989, p.54

If you have to be a monkey, be a

Gorilla

Tierversuche | Bioassays

Schau nit so, sonst bleibt's Dir no

Siebdruck 2006

Don't give me that look - it might not go away!

screen print 2006

Ich bin doch keine Mouse!

Siebdruck 2007

I am not a mouse!

screen print 2007

First I liked Vietnam, now I love Germany

Siebdruck | screen print 2007

m u

mu

Siebdruck | screen print 2005

UN-Soldat gibt Tarnung auf

Siebdruck, coloriert 2007

UN soldier uncovered

screen print, colored 2007

agent lemon

Objekt | object 2004

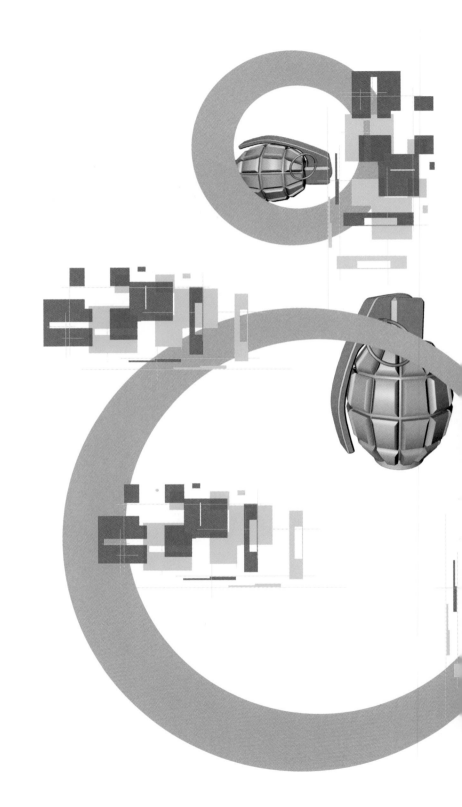

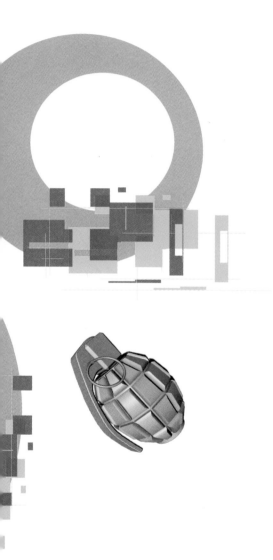

ATTACKE!

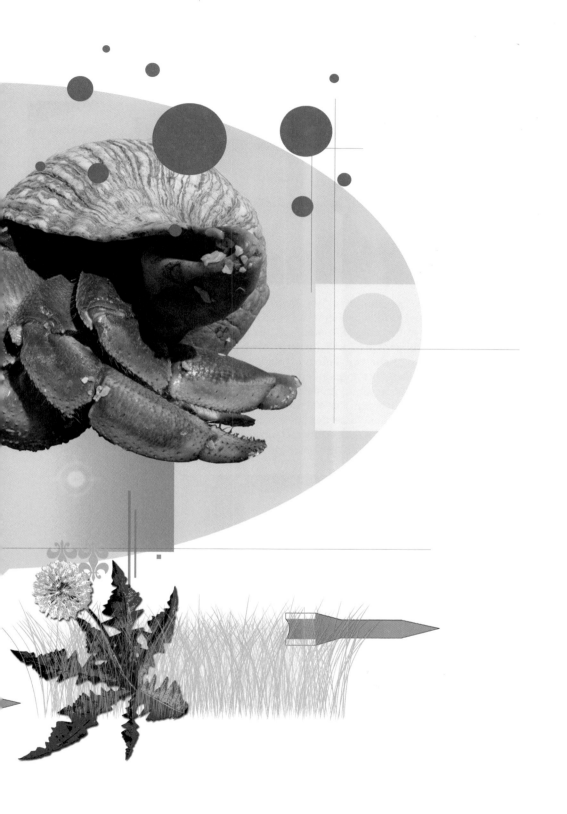

ATTACKE!

Ein Eingriff ins optische Raumklima unter Anleitung von Guy Debord

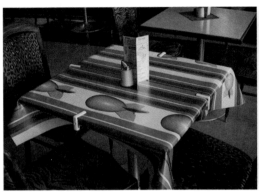

Auf den ersten Blick ein gewöhnliches Café. Jedoch wird man bei näherer Betrachtung gewahr, dass die Tischdecken aus LKW-Planen hergestellt und mit stilisiertem Kriegsmaterial bedruckt sind. Fern jedes Bestrebens, Waffen zu glorifizieren, soll hier die Psychogeographie beeinflusst werden, indem gewohnte, ortsabhängige Bildinhalte verschoben und in einem neuen Kontext präsentiert werden. Das kaffeehaustypische Ambiente und Interieur (Getränke, Gespräche, Zeitschriften) wird mit Hilfe divergierender Elemente angegriffen, attackiert.

In der beschriebenen Situation werden zudem die Gäste wie das Personal des Cafés „Opfer" dieses optischen Angriffs. Debord schreibt: „Die älteste gesellschaftliche Spezialisierung ist [es,] die Spezialisierung der Gewalt, die an der Wurzel des Spektakels liegt".[1]

ATTACKE ist eine situationistische Auseinandersetzung mit Krieg und Gewalt in einem Kontext, der diesen Schrecken eigentlich nicht erwarten ließ. „In der *wirklich verkehrten* Welt ist das Wahre ein Moment des Falschen."[2]

---

1   Debord, Guy: Die Gesellschaft des Spektakels, Hamburg 1978, S. 23
2   Ebd.

ATTACK!

Interference with the visual climate, instructed by Guy Debord

An ordinary café at first sight. Once you get closer, however, you notice that the tablecloths are made of lorry canvas printed with stylized war material. Far from attempting to glorify war, Roland Maurmair tries to influence psycho-geography by shifting familiar images associated with certain places into a new context. The typical atmosphere and interior of a café (drinks, conversations, newspapers) are bombarded, attacked with the aid of diverging elements.
In the situation described, the guests and café staff are "victims" of this visual attack, too.
Debord writes: "The oldest social specialisation, that is the specialisation of power, is at the root of the spectacle".[1]
ATTACK is a situational approach to war, power and violence in a context where such terror is not normally expected. "In a world that is truly inversed, the truth is a moment of untruth."[2]

1   Debord, Guy: The Society of the Spectacle, Hamburg 1978, p. 23
2   ibid.

Die Afrikaner kommen!

Die Afrikaner kommen!

Ein Teil meiner Familie – meine Schwägerin kommt aus Mali, mein Neffe und meine Nichte sind Halb-Malinesen – kommt von jenem Kontinent der Erde, über dem in unserem Bewusstsein oft nach wie vor der Schatten der hegelschen Weltgeschichte liegt.

So erschien im Frühjahr 2005 in der österreichischen „Kronenzeitung" ein Artikel mit der Schlagzeile „Afrikaner im Vormarsch". In bedrohlichem Ton beschrieb der Artikel, wie nordafrikanische Drogendealer, illegal oder verkleidet als Asylwerber, unser Land „überschwemmen".

Viele Plakate der Caritas in Wien – „Ihre Spende lebt" – sind überschmiert mit dem Zusatz „als Drogen-Neger"; als solche nämlich treten Afrikaner in unseren Breiten medial in Erscheinung, wodurch eine paranoide Fremdenfeindlichkeit geschürt wird, die ihren Ausfluss auch in diversen abwertenden Bezeichnungen findet.

Das Projekt „Die Afrikaner kommen!" ist der Versuch, mit künstlerischer Ironie und Humor auf diese paranoide und rassistische Situation zu reagieren. Zu diesem Zweck wurden, nach der Vorlage des gleichnamigen Siebdrucks, kleine Abziehbilder produziert, die in den Städten Innsbruck, Wien, München, Turin, Berlin, Amsterdam und Barcelona im öffentlichen Raum an verschiedenen Stellen angebracht wurden, um die rassistische Situation deutlich zu machen.

Der Siebdruck zeigt eine afrikanische Familie, Mann, Frau und Kinder, die allesamt Koffer in den Händen tragen, worin sich, nein, keine Drogen, sondern ihre letzten Habseligkeiten befinden. Menschen auf der Flucht, Menschen mit der Hoffnung auf ein besseres Leben. Der Himmel ist blau, die Sonne scheint, das Gras ist grün und die Afrikaner kommen.

Die Afrikaner kommen! | The Africans are coming!
Siebdruck | screen print 2005

The Africans are coming!

Part of my family – my sister-in-law from Mali and my nephew and niece who are half-Malian – are from the continent that, in our minds, is still over-shadowed by Hegelian history.

In spring 2005, an article entitled "Africans gaining ground" was published in the Austrian tabloid "Kronenzeitung". The article described in a menacing tone how drug dealers from Northern Africa, as illegal immigrants or disguised as asylum seekers, were "flooding" our country. Many posters in Vienna featuring the slogan *Your donation lives on* to advertise the Caritas charity organisation are defaced with the words *"as drug niggers"*, which is the name that Africans are frequently referred to in the media in Austria. In this way paranoid xenophobia is fuelled, which in turn manifests itself in various derogatory names.

The project *The Africans are coming!* is an attempt to react to this paranoid and racist behaviour with artistic irony and humour. For this purpose, the screen print with the same title was used as a reference to produce stickers, which were stuck in different public places in Innsbruck, Vienna, Munich, Torino, Berlin, Amsterdam and Barcelona to make people aware of the racist situation.

The screenprint shows an African family – father, mother and children – who are all carrying suitcases containing, not drugs, but their last belongings. People on the run, hoping for a better life. The sky is blue, the sun is shining, the grass is green and the Africans are coming.

DoT – Depth of Texture

Die Tiefe der Textur

Die Welt ist erforscht. Innen wie außen, oben wie unten gibt es kaum noch einen unbekannten, nicht definierten Ort. Egal, wohin wir blicken, ob auf ferne Planeten oder durch ein Mikroskop: Beim Vorstoß in unbekanntes Terrain wird, bevor man in tiefere Schichten eindringt, zuerst dessen Oberfläche sondiert. Erreicht man die Grenzen der sensitiven Abtastungsmöglichkeiten, helfen uns technologische Prothesen und mediale Dispositive beim weiteren Wahrnehmen, Erkennen und Verstehen der Wirklichkeit.

Verringert man die Entfernung zum beobachteten Gegenstand, verändert sich automatisch auch die Sichtweise: Dringt man unter die Oberfläche eines betrachteten Objekts, erschließt sich eine mehrschichtige, mehr-dimensionale Struktur, ein Netzwerk aus Hüllen und Schalen, welches wir als unseren physikalischen Raum definieren. Bei noch näherer Betrachtung reduziert sich unsere Realität gar auf ein paar sich ständig bewegende Teilchen, dazwischen: leerer Raum.

Wir geben uns damit zufrieden, uns die Wirklichkeit von zweidimensionalen Bildern eines Rasterelektronenmikroskops oder der US-amerikanischen Marssonde erklären zu lassen, wir generieren die Welt, indem wir sie beschreiben: in Form von Sprache, Text, Bildern und Symbolen. Wir sitzen vor einer zweidimensionalen Mattscheibe und blicken durch sie in eine illusorische Ferne, schwimmen in einem Bilderfluss, der uns Information und Unterhaltung liefert und menschliche Nähe zu vermitteln versucht. Ohne uns dessen bewusst zu sein, haben wir uns eine zusätzliche mediale Haut übergestreift, agieren selbst nur mehr als Interfaces der von uns erfundenen Maschinen, mit Hilfe derer wir unsere abstrakten Ideen, Systeme und Theorien im Virtuellen realisieren, um die Beschaffenheit *der Welt da draußen* zu begreifen. Die in unserem Kopf (der eigentlichen zentralen Steuereinheit) generierten Codes, Programme, Standards und Normen, die die Abläufe unserer Wirklichkeit mathematisch beschreiben, werden ausgelagert und zu externen Steuerungs-, Rechen- und Speichereinheiten. Wenn wir diesen zu viel Verantwortung übertragen, wird es schwierig zu erkennen, wer nun eigentlich was und wer wen unter Kontrolle hat.

Erst vor kurzem wurde der PC in Deutschland zum Teil der persönlichen Intimsphäre erklärt. Gleichzeitig kann in diese, dank des Internets, leichter denn je eingedrungen werden (wie viel sicherer scheint im Vergleich dazu doch das alte Tagebuch!). Damit einher geht auch die Versuchung, diesen potenziellen Nistplatz normabweichenden Gedankenguts zu kontrollieren, denn: Weicht man vom Zentrum ab, gelangt man früher oder später an den Rand, was es, zumindest aus zentraler Perspektive, zu vermeiden gilt – gelangt man doch oft erst in der Ferne zur eigentlichen *Übersicht*, jener Perspektive also, welche von zu großer Nähe des Betrachters zum betrachteten Gegenstand verunmöglicht wird.

Solange man sich im System, oder zumindest nah an dessen Mitte, befindet, ist es schwierig, Aussagen über dessen Beschaffenheit zu treffen; verändert man jedoch seine Position, bzw. verändert man z.B. bestimmte Codes, dann verändert sich das Programm, dessen Ablauf und das System selbst. Die Aussagen, die man bezüglich des Systems treffen wollte, stimmen nicht mehr, weil sich das System selbst verändert hat.

Wir glauben unterscheiden zu können zwischen Akzeptanz und Ablehnung, zwischen Ein- und Ausschluss, zwischen Nähe und Ferne und müssen in diesem Zusammenspiel der Unterschiede doch erkennen, das sich der Raum verdichtet, der Ort und mit ihm die Grenzen verschwinden.

Im urbanen Kontext besitzt der Begriff der Peripherie eine soziokulturelle Relevanz: Die Pariser Vororte, „les banlieues", die wie Kolonien abgeschottet und ghettoisiert von der restlichen Stadtgemeinschaft scheinbar autark eigene Zentren in sich bilden, siedeln örtlich betrachtet an derselben Stelle wie die wohlbehüteten Reichenvierteln, die „gated communities" unserer Großstädte, abseits vom eigentlichen Stadtkern. Bei dieser Disparität stellt sich nicht die Frage, wer ist drinnen und wer draußen, sondern wer ist wo?

Kollabiert eines der urbanen Subsysteme, ist das ganze System betroffen, wie z.B. bei den Ausschreitungen im Jahre 2005 in Clichy-sous-Bois. Was als Auseinandersetzung zwischen der Polizei und drei afrikanischen Jugendlichen begann, weitete sich auf ganz Frankreich aus und bald brannten die Autos im ganzen Land. Auch in anderen europäischen Städten zündeten Jugendliche Fahrzeuge an. Darauf folgte, dass die Integrationsdebatte in ganz Europa aufs Neue medial diskutiert wurde.

Durch die Medialität unserer Gesellschaft ist der Raum enger geworden. Es gibt keinen Ort mehr, der unberührt ist, keinen, der nicht vom verdichteten Informationsfluss erfasst bzw. im Virtuellen generiert wird.

„Der Raum, der einmal ein begehbarer und erfahrbarer Raum und daher ein Raum zum Bereisen war, ist dezentralisiert, differenziert, uneinheitlich, aufgelöst: ein Raum im Fluß. Er ist nirgends und überall, was im globalen elektronischen Zeitalter keine Überraschung ist. Jeder Ort ist so gut wie jeder andere Ort, wenn er nur digital generiert werden kann."[1]

Neues zu entdecken scheint schwierig. Als Ausweg bleibt eine Reise nach Innen, eine Erforschung des Selbst. Ein Exit, das zugleich ein In-it ist. Startet man diesen internen Prozess, stellt man fest, dass das Selbst ein Multiple ist; ein Konglomerat, zusammengesetzt aus Eindrücken, Vorstellungen, Normen, Stimmungen, Sehnsüchten und Wünschen. Auch bei näherem Hinsehen wird kein klares Profil erkennbar. Ein Dilemma. Oder viele.

---

1   Schmidt, Aurel: Von Raum zu Raum, Berlin 1998, S. 90f.

DoT – Depth of Texture

The world is explored. Hardly any place remains unknown and undefined, neither on the inside nor on the outside, neither high above nor down below us. Wherever we look, at remote planets or through a microscope: when we reach unknown territory we first probe the surface before examining deeper layers. Whenever we reach our limits of sensory sampling, we use technical prostheses and other media as a means to further perceive, identify and understand reality. By changing the distance between you and the object you are observing, your perspective automatically changes. Once the surface of the object under observation is broken, a multi-layered, multi-dimensional structure, a network of envelopes and shells that we define as our physical space, unfolds. Upon closer inspection, our reality is reduced even further to a few constantly moving particles – and between them: empty space.

We content ourselves with explanations of reality by way of two-dimensional pictures of a scanning electron microscope or the US-Mars probe; we generate the world by describing it: with the aid of language, text, pictures and symbols. Sat in front of a two-dimensional screen, we look through it into an illusionary distance, swimming in a sea of images trying to provide us with information, entertainment and interpersonal relationships. Without realizing it, we have put on a second media skin, interacting as mere interfaces of the machines we have invented and that help us put into practice our abstract ideas, systems and theories in a virtual world in order to understand the world *out there*. The codes, programmes, standards and norms that are generated in our minds (the actual central unit of control) to mathematically describe the processes taking place in our reality are transferred to external units of control, calculation and storage. When we shift too much responsibility to these units, it becomes more and more difficult to be sure who controls whom or what.

Not long ago, the PC was declared part of each individual's personal privacy. Thanks to the Internet, however, it has become easier than ever before to intrude on this part of privacy (how much safer does the old diary now seem!). Of course, we also feel tempted to control this potential nesting site for thoughts diverging from the norm; by moving away from the centre you will, sooner or later, reach the fringe, which, at least from the central point of view, you should not – as it is only from a certain distance that the observer can gain an actual overview, i.e. the perspective that is impossible to gain when standing too close to the object observed.

While you are at, or at least near the centre of the system, it is difficult to analyse its structure; by changing position, however, or maybe certain codes, the programme, its sequence and the system itself start to change. The analyses of the system no longer hold true given that the system itself has changed.

We believe ourselves to be able to distinguish between acceptance and refusal, between inclusion and exclusion, between proximity and distance; however, we must realize in this interaction of differences that the space compresses and the place disappears, and with it its clearly definable borders.

In an urban context, the word periphery bears a certain socio-cultural relevance. In terms of location, the outskirts of Paris, "les banlieues", which, isolated like colonies and ghettoised by the rest of the city, seem to be self-sufficient, separate centres, are in the same area as the well-guarded quarters of the rich, the so-called gated communities in our cities outside the actual city centre. This disparity does not raise the question of who is inside and who is outside, rather who is where?

When one of these urban sub-systems collapses, the entire system is affected, as was the case in the riots in Clichy-sous-Bois, France in 2005. What started as a conflict between the police and three African youths, quickly spread all over France, and soon cars around the country were on fire. Teenagers in other European countries also began to set fire to cars, as a result of which the integration debate was taken up again by the media in all of Europe.

Due to the media presence in our society, space has become more limited. There is no place left that remains untouched, none that remains unpolluted by the dense flow of information or that is not generated virtually.

"Places that used to be accessible and tangible, and could therefore be explored, are now decentralised, differentiated, incongruent, dissolved: flowing places. Places are nowhere and everywhere, which is not surprising in our global electronic age. Each place is as good as another as long as it can be generated digitally."[1]

It seems difficult to make new discoveries. The only way out is the way inwards to explore ourselves. A way out that is a way in. Once you get this internal process started, you realize that your self is a multiple: a conglomerate of impressions, ideas, norms, moods, longings and desires. Even when looking it at more closely, no clear profile is discernible. A dilemma. Or many.

---

1   Aurel Schmidt: Von Raum zu Raum (From Space to Space), Berlin 1998, p. 90 et seq.

Sind wir nicht alle ein bisschen endo?

Klanginstallation 2000

Dieses Projekt ist Otto E. Rössler, Professor für Chaostheorie in Tübingen, dem Begründer der Endophysik, gewidmet. Seine Forschungen in diesem Grenzbereich der Wissenschaft dienten als Inspirationsquelle und gaben den Anstoß zur Realisierung dieser Idee.

Von Filzkokons ummantelte Audioboxen beschallen einen Raum. Ein Kästchen mit der Aufschrift „Exit", welches für den Besucher frei zugängliche Ohrenstöpsel enthält, befindet sich ebenfalls im Raum; öffnet man es, wird es von innen beleuchtet, gleichzeitig verdunkelt sich der Raum. Das Audiomaterial bilden private Gespräche. Dient der Filz einmal als verhüllende Fassade, steht er zugleich für die semipermeable Schnittstelle, die dem Besucher „akustische Einblicke" in die Intimsphäre der Sprecher zulässt. Das Ohr wird voyeuristisch und die Weichheit des Materials zu einer Metapher für den offensichtlich dünnen Grenzbereich zwischen privat und öffentlich.

Nicht zuletzt förderte das Internet jenes gesellschaftliche Phänomen, welches für die heimelige Abkapselung von der Außenwelt steht und als „Cocooning" bezeichnet wird. Unsere sozialen Kontakte erfahren eine Veränderung, mitunter Verzerrung, wenn, unter Verzicht auf jegliche physische Kommunikation, der Kontakt zur Außenwelt nur noch virtuell über teleauto-matische Schnittstellen hergestellt wird. Die Grenzen zwischen Virtualität und Realität verschwimmen, eine nur bedingt kontrollierbare Infoflut bricht über uns herein, unsere Wahrnehmungswirklichkeit verändert sich – die von allen postulierte Mobilität endet jedoch mit der Kapazität von Server und Akku.

Diese Arbeit unterstreicht die Relevanz traditioneller Kommunikationsformen und ist zugleich eine Hommage an die Kunst des Zuhörens. Der Besucher erhält kurzfristig den Status des Exobeobachters, umgeben von einer Modellwelt und doch Gefangener unserer Wirklichkeit. Die Fragen, die diese Zerrissenheit provoziert, können nur im Inneren beantwortet werden – denn nur dort können die nötigen Informationen über den eigenen Zustand abgerufen werden.

Also doch.

Aren't we all a little bit endo?

sound installation 2000

This project is dedicated to Otto E. Rössler, professor of Chaos Theory in Tübingen, Germany, and founder of endophysics. His research within this marginal discipline served as a source of inspiration to put this idea into practice.

Audio boxes wrapped in felt cocoons fill the room with sound. A box labelled Exit containing earplugs that are at the visitors' free disposal is attached to one of the walls. When opened, it is illuminated from within while simultaneously the room itself gets dark. The audio material consists of intimate private conversations. On the one hand, the felt is a cover protecting the content from sight, while on the other hand it serves as a semi-permeable interface that provides "acoustic insight" to the visitor. The ear turns voyeuristic, the softness becoming metaphorical for the seemingly thin border between privacy and public domain.

The Internet, in particular, has been at the origin of the social phenomenon called cocooning, which refers to individuals shutting themselves off from the world by retreating into their homes. Of course, our social contacts are also changing, sometimes even deforming, when our only contact to the world out there takes place on a virtual level via tele-automatic interfaces without any physical form of communication. The borders between virtual and factual realities begin to blur, we are inundated with a flood of information that can only partly be controlled, and our perception of reality is starting to change – the global buzzword "mobility" ends with the capacity of our servers and batteries.

This work underlines the importance of traditional forms of communication, honouring the art of listening to others. For a short period, the visitor is put into the position of an external observer who is surrounded by a model world, yet imprisoned by reality. The questions triggered by this disparity can only be answered in each visitor's own mind, since that is where the necessary information about one's own state of mind lies.

Yes, we are.

Wir haben alles unter Kontrolle

Maurmairs Kaninchen

Otto E. Rössler

Für J.O.R

Als ich einmal mit dem Auto, einen Zweijährigen am Rücksitz, an einem Gebäude mit öffentlich finanziertem Kunstwerk davor vorbeifuhr, fragte mich dieser: „Was ist das?" Ich sagte: „Kunst." Darauf die Frage: „Was ist Kunst?" Ich antwortete nach einer unfreiwilligen Pause: „Kunst ist es, wenn es ein Witz ist." Die Antwort wurde akzeptiert, als wäre sie final. Alles, was sich dem Kind seitdem jemals in Frage stellte, war von nun an Kunst.

Die Ultraperspektive ist etwas, über das nur Menschen verfügen: Die Eigenschaft, mit dem Herzen des Anderen zu sehen. Kunst bedient sich dieses menschlichen Vorzugs, um den Betrachter emotional zu berühren. Der Witz, in seinem Minimalismus und seiner Effizienz, ist die Kunst der lehrreichen Offenbarung.

Ultraperspektive und Endophysik: Zwei neue Umschreibungen von Kunst, ein Witz in beiden Fällen, – der Witz, in diese Welt geworfen zu sein, und der Witz dieses temporären Moments, der niemals endet. Der Witz wirft mich so heftig aus der Balance, dass ich nur noch wie ein Kind lächeln kann. ABC-Bücher für Kinder – „Le boeuf, der Ochs, la vache, die Kuh, fermez la porte, die Tür mach zu" – sind durchaus feinsinnige Kunst. Sie erfassen dich dort, wo du gerade bist und ziehen dich in einen wirbelnden Tanz hinein, um das Jetzt als die einzige Realität zu feiern. Mit Lächeln und Gelächter und vielleicht ein paar Krokodilstränen am Schluss. Als Personen verstehen wir und werden verstanden. Güte und Witz und Kunst werden möglich. Die Zukunft kann gesichert werden, mildtätige Gerechtigkeit verwirklicht, die nächste Hungersnot verhindert werden, Jean Ziegler lebt nicht vergebens. Mozarts Infantilität ist tief. Händels Hallelujah ist gleichermaßen kitschig und heilig. Wir sind alle kleine Kaninchen. Die Grinsekatze ist in uns, die Substanz des Lächelns.
Alles ist okay, alles wird gut! Danke, Roland M.!

Dein Otto E.

Everything is under Control

Maurmair's rabbits

Otto E. Rössler

For J.O.R

With a two-year-old on the back seat, I was once driving past a building with publicly financed works of art on display when he suddenly asked me, "What is that?" and I said, "Art." He asked again, "What is art?" and I replied, after a short involuntary pause, "Art is when it is a joke." The answer was accepted as if it was absolutely final. Everything the boy has questioned since then has been written off as art.

Ultra-perspective is the capability of human beings to look at the world through someone else's heart. Art makes use of this human virtue in order to be able to reach the observer. A joke, as minimalistic and efficient as it is, is the art of provoking revelations in an instructive way.

Ultra-perspective and endophysics: Two new names given to art, a joke in both cases: the joke of having been thrown into this world, and the joke of this temporary moment that will never end. The joke throws me off balance so violently that I can only smile like a child. Children's alphabet books – I is for Ibis, who felt very ill, so she went to the doctor and asked for a pill – are truly fine art. They meet you where you are, drawing you into a wild dance to celebrate the present as the only reality existing. Smiling and laughing, maybe even shedding a few tears towards the end. As human beings, we understand and are understood. Kindness, joke and art become possible. The future can be saved, benevolent justice can be brought and the next famine prevented. Jean Ziegler's life is not in vain. Mozart's infantility is deeply rooted. Händel's hallelujah is equally kitschy and sacred. We are all little rabbits. We all have the Cheshire cat in us, grinning being the substance of smiling. Everything is ok, everything is going to be alright!
Thank you, Roland M.!

Yours, Otto E.

Rabbitism

Manfred Faßler

… das Ziel im Rücken, rückversichernd, vorausschauend nachschauend, auf Gegenverkehr, Weggabelungen, Straßennamen und auf die Unversehrtheit seiner Last achtend, bemüht sich ein Mensch, andeutungsweise versteckt hinter einer schnell geschnittenen weißen Hasenmaske, eine überdimensionale Möhre in seinen Bau zu bekommen. Von Anfang an entspinnt sich ein kurioses Wechselspiel von Hasenmensch und Möhrensack: der rückwärts laufende Hase, minimalistisch inszenierte Kurzgeschichte über, ja über was eigentlich?

Wer Roland Maurmair kennt, weiß, dass es ihm oft genug darum geht, Sprachbilder und Bildsprachen zu zerlegen, die Metaphorik mit ihrer Unmöglichkeit zu konfrontieren, haltbare Aussagen oder Zeichensprachen zu entwickeln. Er zeigt jene immer wieder genutzte und darum nicht klüger werdende Haltlosigkeit der Sprache auf, unterläuft sie mit Bildern, mit zeichnerischen Kleinodien und beweist damit die Aussagestärke des Bildes, das nicht mit der Attitüde der Scheinschwangerschaft kommender Wichtigkeit daherkommt. Es ist die Friedfertigkeit der Person Roland Maurmair, die die Kraft gibt, eben nicht draufzuhauen, sondern draufzuschauen. Er zerlegt die Unbedachtheit des Alltags und institutionellen Hochmutes in bedenkenswerte Details, leistet im Kleinen einen radikalen Umbau des sehenden Denkens.

Irgendwann hieß es chaostheoretisch, dass ein leichter Flügelschlag eines Schmetterlings im Amazonasgebiet durch positive Verstärkungen zum Wirbelsturm über dem Nordatlantik führen könnte. Nun, erlebt haben wir es noch nicht, aber denkbar ist es, dass Roland Maurmair solche leichten Flügelschläge in Tirol oder Wien erzeugt. Wem dann die Maske wegfliegt, weiß ich nicht.
Ach ja, die Maske, der Mensch, die Möhre und Wien. Der Mensch, maskiert als Hase und mit einer Last versehen, die ihm Mühe bereitet, verlässt das Feld- und Waldareal, durchstreift in einer gezielten Annäherung die vorstädtischen Regionen, Ecken, Engpässe, vermeidet Zusammenstöße mit Automasken des Menschen, und überlebt. Er schleppt sich und seine Aufgabe vom Land in die Stadt, von der Wiese auf das Kopfsteinpflaster, vom namenlosen Gelände zur namentlichen Adresse: 10. Bezirk, Hasengasse. Das Register aus Zahl, Topologie und Namen wirkt dümmlich, lächerlich gegenüber der namenlosen Herkunft. Tierische Freude kommt auch nicht auf. Der Menschhase, voll seinem unheimlichen Auftrag gewidmet, weiß, wohin er muss, denn das Wort, das Versprechen der Adresse ist zwingend. Wo Hasengasse draufsteht, dort lass dich, Hase, nieder. Der Mensch versteht sich auf falsche Etiketten, auf etikettierte Fälschung. Und hier arbeitet das Erzählspiel mit Zeilensprüngen. Weder Mensch noch Hasenmaske, der merkwürdige Sack und eine Möhre, die karge Straße und der Straßenname passen so richtig zusammen.

Man wartet auf die Rückkehr aus dem Hauseingang, auf den Rücken, hinter dem der Möhrensack wieder aus der Namensfalle herausgezogen wird. Nichts geschieht. Nach Sekunden merkt man, dass es diesem Kleinod gelungen ist, dass ich als Betrachter dem Weg des Hasen nachsinne, den Wegen des Menschen nachsinne, der mit so viel vermeintlich täuschenden Ähnlichkeiten sich blind tapeziert, wo es weder die Ähnlichkeiten noch die Täuschungen wirklich gibt. Denn wir produzieren Unpassendes. Und Roland Maurmair ist der Entzauberer, der ohne Las Vegas-Show dem Denken wieder Spielräume gibt. Was wir daraus machen, ist unsere Sache … nur grinsen sollte man dabei, über sich, über andere, auch lachen über so viele Lebensdetails, die wir schöngeredet, d.h. symbolisch verklärt haben. Es ist diese leise Selbstironie, die durch seine Arbeiten entsteht, ohne Zeigefinger, ohne Boshaftigkeit, sondern mit der Sensibilität und Klarheit und mit dem Mut, auch rückwärts vorwärts zu gehen, denn wir wissen nie, was kommt, aber sollten im Auge behalten, was wir mitnehmen.

Rabbitism:

Jede Person oder Sache, deren Handeln, Erscheinen, Verhalten und Instinkte nach ihrer Art und Form durch und durch und völlig unzweideutig hasenhaft sind.

Rabbitism

Manfred Faßler

With his goal at his rear, reassuring himself, looking ahead by looking back, cautiously paying attention to the oncoming traffic, intersections, street names, and holding onto his load, a man, in part hidden behind a quickly cut white rabbit mask, tries to get an oversized carrot into his burrow. From the very beginning, a strange interplay develops between the rabbit man and the carrot sack: the rabbit moving backward, a minimalistically staged short story about – well, what exactly?

Those familiar with Roland Maurmair know that his work is quite often about dissecting metaphors and visual languages, confronting metaphorics with its impossibility, developing tenable statements or symbolic languages. He shows the oft-used instability of language, which becomes none the cleverer with repetition, and subverts it with language, with drawn miniature gems or thus shows the power of the image that does not pretend any future importance. It is Roland Maurmair's reticence as a person that gives him the power not to loudly pronounce his message, but to look up toward it. He dissects the carelessness of everyday life and institutional arrogance in striking details, achieving a radical reconstruction of visual thought in miniature. At some point, chaos theory claimed that the slightest motion of a butterfly wing in the Amazon could trigger a hurricane over the North Atlantic through positive amplification. Now, although we haven't experienced it yet, it's conceivable that Roland Maurmair could generate such light flaps of the wing in Tyrol or Vienna. But I don't know whose mask will be blown off by it.

Ah yes, the mask, man, carrots, and Vienna. Man, masked as a rabbit and given a heavy burden, leaves field and forest, with a goal in mind walks through the suburban regions, corners, narrow passages, avoids collisions with the car-masks of the individuals, and somehow survives. He drags himself and his burden from the countryside to the city, from the field to the cobblestones, from nameless terrain to a named address: Vienna, 10th District, Hasengasse, or „Rabbit Lane." The register of number, topology, and name seems stupid, laughable vis-à-vis the nameless place of origin. Animalistic joy does not come to pass. The man-rabbit is fully dedicated to his uncanny task, and knows where he must go, for the word, the promise of the address is compelling. If the place is called „rabbit lane," then this is where the rabbit must settle. Man understands false labels, labeled falsification. The narrative game works by skipping lines. Neither person nor rabbit mask, the strange sack and a carrot, the bare street and the street name really fit together.

We await the return from the house entrance, on its back, behind which the sack of carrots is again pulled from the trap of the name. But nothing happens. After a few seconds, it is noticed that this gem has succeeded in making me think as beholder about the path of the rabbit, the paths of man who with so many supposed deceiving similarities wallpapers himself blind, where there are neither similarities nor deceptions. For we produce the unfitting. And Roland Maurmair is the disenchanter, who without any Las Vegas show again gives thinking room to maneuver. What we make of that is our own matter... At any event, one should grin while doing so, about oneself, about others, laugh about so details of life that we have talked up, that is, symbolically romanticized. It is this quiet self-irony that emerges through his works, without an index finger, without ill will, but with sensitivity, and clarity, and with the courage to also move backwards, for we never know what's coming, but should keep an eye on what we take with us.

Rabbitism:

Any person or thing whose actions, appearance, behaviors and instincts are quintessentially and unequivocally rabbit-like in nature and form.

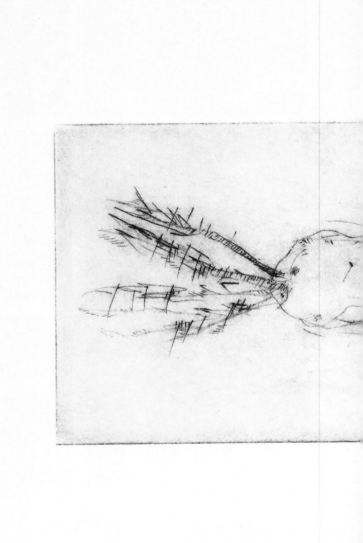

Rabbitism" Jon Altman 2007

Ein Häuschen im Grauen

Zwischen Traum und Albtraum; eine Annäherung an das unendliche Thema vom Leben auf begrenztem Raum.

Welcher Stadtmensch träumt nicht von einem Häuschen im Grünen?
Und das nicht erst seit sich unsere urbane Lebenswelt fortschreitend als technisiert, automatisiert, schnell und virtuell offenbart. Zwar erschließen wir ständig neue virtuelle Räume und digitalisieren gleichzeitig unsere reale Lebenswelt mit der Intention, sie damit zu bewahren, vernachlässigen dabei aber die Wahrnehmungswirklichkeit unserer alltäglichen, realen Umgebung. Indes verwahrlosen die Städte zu einer, der motorisierten Bewegung unterworfenen, Konstruktion aus Transiträumen, deren fahle Ausstrahlung uns kein Zuhause mehr zu bieten vermag. Die Flucht vorm Alltag endet zunehmend in medialen und virtuellen Welten, wo wir glauben, ein neues Zuhause für uns entdecken zu können.

Ebenso begeben wir uns nach wie vor gerne in Erholung und Regeneration suggerierende „Pause-Zonen", wie Gärten oder Parkanlagen. Dabei stört es uns nicht, dass es sich um eine von Landschaftsarchitekten gestaltete, künstliche Natur handelt; im Gegenteil scheint sie unsere Entspannungsbedürfnisse vollständig zu befriedigen. Eine Pseudonatur, die sich uns als „authentischer Lebensraum" anbiedert, hat sich als Alternative zur Ungastlichkeit[1] des urbanen Betondschungels etabliert. Ist es die städtische Anonymität, die dem *Grauen* die Chance sich auszubreiten bietet, vor dem wir dann die Flucht ins (vermeintlich) Natürliche und Ländliche antreten?

Nicht erst seit die Aktivitäten von Franz Fuchs und Josef Fritzl öffentlich wurden, wissen wir, dass um nichts weniger als in der Stadt auch am Land die kranken Geschichten ihre Heimstatt haben, dass in den Kellern der Vorstadthäuser nicht nur Kartoffeln und Wein gelagert werden und dass im Schutz der netten Nachbarschaft auch so einiges verborgen bleibt. Die häufig suggerierte Stadt-Land-Dichotomie scheint folglich nicht zu greifen. Schwärmen wir einerseits vom Charme des Ländlichen, müssen wir doch zugeben, dass uns die Stadt Potenziale ganz anderer Art zu bieten vermag.

Ähnlich ambivalent verhält es sich mit der Idylle und dem Grauen, bereitet uns das Grauen doch zuweilen sogar Vergnügen; wir holen es uns nach Hause, denke man an die Medien, die uns tagtäglich mit Schreckensnachrichten auf dem Laufenden halten oder an gewaltverherrlichende Filme und Videospiele, die wir konsumieren. Aggression, Hass, Gewalt und Terror scheinen genauso zum Menschsein zu gehören wie die Liebe oder die Sehnsucht nach Frieden.

Neben den besprochenen realen wie virtuellen Erholungsarealen gestalten wir uns ein Zuhause, in welchem wir versuchen, eine Idylle zu implementieren, die immer wieder wie eine Seifenblase zu platzen droht. Der letzte Wirtschaftscrash verstärkte noch die Tendenz zu einer neuen, biedermeierischen Häuslichkeit. Es bleibt zu hoffen, dass bei diesem Rückzug in die eigenen vier Wände nur Ikeamöbel, und keine Bomben, zusammengebaut werden.

---

1   Vgl. Mitscherlich, Alexander: Die Unwirtlichkeit unserer Städte. Anstiftung zum Unfrieden. Frankfurt/Main 1965

LOS QUEREMOS A TODOS...

¡PRESOS!

ESTOS SON LOS DELINCUENTES MÁS BUSCADOS, SI LOS CONOCE O LOS HA VISTO

¡¡DENÚNCIELOS!!

Wo ist das Heim, das uns vor dem Grauen schützt – im Mutterschoß dem Ort, wo noch alles in Ordnung ist? Der erste Schock ist die Geburt. Einmal hinausgepresst in eine kalte, grelle Welt versuchen wir uns zu orientieren und suchen eine neue Bleibe. Wir sehnen uns nach Ordnung und verlässlichen Mustern und Instrumenten zur Wirklichkeitsinterpretation. Wir teilen ein, verzeichnen, speichern und sortieren. Wir benennen, bestimmen und kategorisieren. Wir beherrschen – die Natur in Form von Topfpflanzen, Parkanlagen und Tiergärten. Bis hin zur Gentechnologie gelingt es uns, der Natur ins Handwerk zu pfuschen – nicht zuletzt um dieser Naturgewalt die Stirn bieten zu können, die Natur zu zähmen, indem wir zur Peitsche der Kultur greifen.

A country cottage
surrounded by grey shadows

Dream or nightmare; approaching the never-ending story of life within limits.

Who wouldn't dream of a nice little country cottage surrounded by green grass and trees? This is a phenomenon that started long before our urban life began to rapidly become more mechanized, automated, hurried and virtual. We have been creating new virtual space and digitalizing real life in order to preserve it; however, in the process we have been neglecting the reality of perception of our true daily surroundings. At the same time, cities are being reduced to a construction of transitory dreams subject to motorized movement whose dead atmosphere does not offer us a home any longer. Our escape from the daily grind ends more and more often in virtual media worlds, where we believe to have found a new home.

Likewise, we enjoy spending our time in "break zones" suggesting recreation and regeneration. We do not mind that nature in these gardens has been created artificially by landscape gardeners; on the contrary, they seem to completely satisfy our need for relaxation. Some kind of pseudo-nature, presenting itself to us as an "authentic habitat", has established itself as an alternative to the inhospitality1 of the urban concrete jungle. Is it anonymity that makes it possible for the grey shadows to spread, which we then try to escape by fleeing into (supposedly) natural and rural space?

We've known for quite some time, even since before the horrors perpetrated by Franz Fuchs and Josef Fritzl became public, that sick stories are home not only to urban but also to rural areas, where not only potatoes and wine are stored in the cellars, and quite a few things remain hidden from the neighbors. The dichotomy between the country and the city does not seem to apply here. While enthusing about the charm of country life, we simultaneously must admit that only the city can offer us the opportunities that the countryside does not provide.
There is a similar ambivalence about idyll and horror, as we sometimes even enjoy the horror; we even let it into our homes, via the media, for instance, which bring us home the latest horrible news every day, or by consuming violence-glorifying films and video games. Aggression, hatred, violence and terror seem to be part of us as are love and the longing for peace.

Besides spending our time in both the real and virtual recreational areas described above, we create a home where we attempt to implement an idyll that continuously threatens to burst like a bubble. The last economic crisis even reinforced the tendency towards a new conservative and domestic lifestyle. Hopefully, this withdrawal will merely lead people to build IKEA furniture and not bombs.

---

1   Cf. Mitscherlich, Alexander: Die Unwirtlichkeit unserer Städte. Anstiftung zum Unfrieden. (Our cities' inhospitality. Sparking unrest.) Frankfurt/Main 1965

Where is the home that protects us from these grey shadows – the mother's womb where everything is still all right? Birth is the first shock. Once we have been pushed out into a cold and bright world we try to orient ourselves and look for a new place to stay. We long for order, reliable patterns, and instruments to interpret reality. We classify, file, save and order. We label, define and categorize. We control – nature with our potted plants, parks and zoos. Gene technology is our ultimate masterpiece of interfering with nature – not least to defy nature by taming it with the whip of culture.

Invasion of
the Cyber Crickets

Medieninstallation 2007/2009

Durch den Umbau von Erinnerungsgeräten für die Medikamenteneinnahme, kam es in den Aus-
stellungsräumen zu einer Invasion von 200 kleinen zirpenden Grillen. Die Installation wurde 2007
in New Orleans, 2008 in Innsbruck und 2009 in Wien in unterschiedlichen Versionen präsentiert.

media installation 2007/2009

Maurmair launched an invasion of 200 little chirping crickets by remodelling microchips designed to remind you to take your meds. The installation was presented in various versions in New Orleans in 2007, in Innsbruck in 2008 and in Vienna in 2009.

DIFENDI
LA NATURA

non lasciare
questo   in giro
           sacchetto

- riutilizzalo più volte
  per la tua spesa
  e, quindi,
  come contenitore
  per rifiuti domestici.
- Non abbandonarlo
  nell'ambiente.
  Questo sacchetto

Subversive Codes

Tereza Kotyk

Ist die beste Subversion nicht die, Codes zu entstellen, statt sie zu zerstören?
Roland Barthes

Roland Barthes' Zitat steht für die aktivistische Arbeit der Kommunikationsguerilla, die eine künstlerische Strategie zur Subversion darstellt. Ähnlich dem Anarchismus, Situationismus, den frühen Avantgarde-Bewegungen und der Hackerkultur verwendet sie die künstlerische und parodierte Bearbeitung von bekannten Texten, Bildern und Zeichen als Mittel zum Zweck der Entlarvung: der eigenen Erwartungshaltung wird der Spiegel vorgesetzt, das Alltägliche durch Verzerrung erschüttert, der eingeübte Gehorsam vor Autoritäten bewusst gemacht.

Diese bewusste Auseinandersetzung mit codiertem Verhalten und Systemen ist Ausgangspunkt und Ziel der graphischen Arbeiten von Roland Maurmair. Er bedient sich ähnlicher Methoden wie jener der Kommunikationsguerilla, liegt als Künstler auf der Lauer, irritiert die Erwartungshaltung und schafft Verwirrung, wenn er vertraute Sprüche und Bilder aus ihrem gewohnten Zusammenhang reißt und sie in einen neuen Kontext stellt. Um das zu erreichen, bleibt er nicht im jeweiligen Medium selbst haften, sondern setzt bei der Zeichnung an, ergänzt diese mit installativen Elementen oder photografischen Arbeiten und kombiniert Mischtechniken wie Kartoffeldruck, Kaffeemalerei und Sprayen mit Schablonen.

In *Nest* (2006), hat Maurmair eine graphische Arbeit über den Papierrand in das Kaufhaus Tyrol in Innsbruck wachsen lassen, indem er Zeichnungen von Ratten über Wände, Kartons, Kisten, Säcke und den Boden wandern ließ. In einem Plastiksack mit der Aufforderung „Difendi la Natura" verursachte zusätzlich ein kleiner Motor ein Rascheln im Papier.
Die „Natur zu verteidigen" ist eine Aufforderung zur Initiative, dessen Intention die Ratten entgegenstehen: Die Ratten sind ein Symbol für eine Scheinwelt, an der genagt wird, bis sie eines Tages ausgehöhlt zusammenfällt. Die Ratten haben gewissermaßen an diesem temporär für einen Umbau leer stehenden Haus genagt und in diesen lebensfeindlichen Bedingungen eine Revolution von unten angezettelt. Ratten als Widerstandskämpfer vor dem finalen Zusammenbruch eines Hauses, das einst als modernstes Kaufhaus Westösterreichs im Zweiten Weltkrieg arisiert wurde.

Die Afrikaner kommen! (2005), ist wiederum eine Arbeit, bei welcher der Künstler Reproduktionen seines gleichnamigen Siebdrucks im öffentlichen Raum installierte: Auf dem originalen, bunten und plakativen Siebdruck sind „afrikanische" Männer, Frauen und Kinder mit Koffern abgebildet, die sich auf einer Reise befinden und auf der Suche nach dem richtigen „Ankommen" sind. Mit diesem Siebdruck werden Begriffe wie Migration, Hoffnung, Familie und Vertreibung assoziiert: In manchen österreichischen Zeitungen wurden in den letzten Jahren MigrantInnen und vor allem AfrikanerInnen in höchstem Maße vorverurteilt und mit Vorurteilen besetzt, welchen es in einer österreichischen, muffig-rassistischen Atmosphäre besonders gut zu gedeihen und zu wachsen gelang – wie es beispielsweise Alois Brandstetter in seinem Text „Der 1. Neger meines Lebens" beschreibt: Das Erbe eines alten Hegel'schen Denkens, das den fremden und tierähnlichen Charakter des Negers beweisen möchte und dessen Vorurteile sich unserem Denken einverleibt haben.[1]

---

1   Zaunschirm, Thomas: Das Tier im Menschen – was sind Taubstumme und Neger?, in: Kunstforum International, Im Zoo der Kunst II, Band 175, Ruppichteroth April-Mai 2005, S. 71f.

Maurmair hat kleine Abziehbilder von dem originalen Siebdruck produziert, die in den Städten Innsbruck, Wien, München, Turin, Berlin, Amsterdam und Barcelona im öffentlichen Raum angebracht wurden. Der Siebdruck wurde so zum Teil eines Ganzen, das als inhaltliche Aussage die einzelnen Straßen und Städte miteinander verbunden hat und sich in der Gesamtheit der Aktion als radikale Absage an jedwede Form des Rassismus verstand. Plakativ werden solche Vorurteile postuliert; Maurmair antwortete darauf mit den gleichen Mitteln.

Im Gegensatz zur Verachtung und dem Hass auf den „fremden und tierähnlichen" Menschen steht die allgemeine Liebe zum Tier selbst. Maurmair verwendet daher nicht nur Klischeebilder unserer menschlichen Vorurteile, sondern auch Bilder und Comics von Tieren: Biene Maya, Micky Mouse, Ziege, Koala Bär, Panda, Schildkröte, Schlange, Tausendfüßler, Schweine, Hasen, Enten, Gürteltier, Ratten, Kühe, Giraffe etc. finden sich als Sujet in seinen graphischen Arbeiten. Seine Tiere werden mit menschlichen Eigenschaften „überschrieben", verfremdet und mit einer ironischen Verschiebung unterlegt, die er in den Titeln festhält. Sie haben persönliche, soziale, philosophische Probleme, sind verliebt oder gebrochenen Herzens, – wie ein Gürteltier, das auf Äußerlichkeiten fixiert ist und sich in eine Handgranate verliebt (*Untitled*, 2006; siehe auch: *Ich Jane, du Tarzan*, 2008).

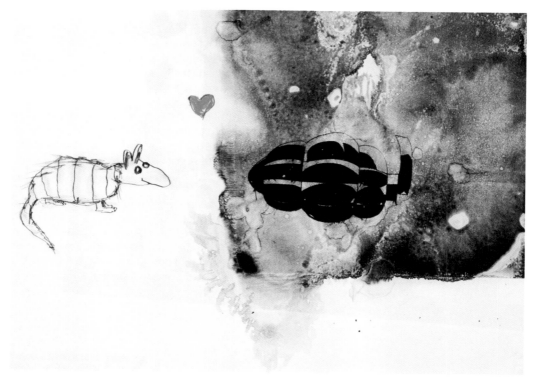

Sie stehen unter Strom oder sind dem Tode nahe, sehen sich vor politischen und scheinbar nicht zu überbrückenden Problemen (*Lately in Ramallah*, 2004). Das Bild des Hasen taucht immer wieder auf: In den meisten dieser Arbeiten kämpft der Hase beständig mit seinem medial aufgeladenen Bild des Helden, wie dem batteriebetriebenen Duracell-Hasen (*His Master's Voice*, 2009; *Natural Amplifier* 2007; *Blind Date III*, 2006; *Blind Date II*, 2005) oder wird Teil einer performativen Aktion im öffentlichen Raum (*Rabbitism*, 2007).

In seiner druckgraphischen Serie *Helden der Kindheit* sind es die tragischen Momente, die der Künstler ins Satirische überzeichnet. Er greift dabei die Idee des tragischen Helden auf, die er im Alltag, in den Medien oder in Bildern seiner eigenen Kindheit verortet. Maurmair bezieht sich auch auf die „Sinnsprüche", die uns Menschen durch den Alltag führen und unserem Leben Sinn geben sollen. *Wenn Du glaubst, es geht nicht mehr, kommt von irgendwo ein Lichtlein her* (2009) ist dann auch der Titel einer der Arbeiten Maurmairs, welche zeigt wie „Klopfer", der Hase aus der Disney-Erzählung „Bambi", eben diesem hinterrücks den Wedel anzündet. *Wenn ich groß bin, werde ich Bildungsbudget* (2010) ist eine weitere Arbeit, die einen glücklichen Pumuckl – der in der Hängematte von der Zukunft träumt und 0 + 1 zu 2 zusammenzählt – zeigt, während in *free your ass, your mind will follow* (2009) Puh, der Bär, seiner angestauten Laune rückwärtig Luft verschafft.

In dieser Form der humoristischen Verschiebung finden sich Aussagen auf verschiedenen Ebenen: einerseits auf der des Sujets und dessen Aufforderung (Sprechblase) und andererseits auf der Ebene der Definition in den Titeln (Schrift). Maurmairs menschelnde Tiergestalten sind unserer Existenz sehr nahe – in ihrer Zerbrechlichkeit und Verletzbarkeit, in ihrer Ausgesetztheit, Verwirrtheit und Wut, in ihrem Begehren, ihrer Illusionsschwelgerei und ihrem hoffnungsgeladenen Zukunftsstreben.

Das „Tier" dient einem metaphorisch-symbolhaften Umweg, um zum Menschen zu gelangen. Insbesondere die bereits erwähnten „Ratten" und ihre subversive Strategie, sich guerillahaft die Straße und die Stadt als Lebensraum anzueignen, fungieren als Symbole des Widerstands. In den Darstellungen derselben wird das Moment der politischen Aussage im Spannungsfeld zwischen „high culture" und „mass culture" weitergeführt (*Bienvenido, negrito!*, 2006).

Bereits Walter Benjamin erkannte den revolutionären Charakter dieser Verknüpfung von Linie, Zeichnung und Humor als subversives Mittel zur Aufhebung codierten Verhaltens[2] und veröffentlichte 1928 das Buch „Die Einbahnstraße", das in der „Sprache der Straße" verfasst ist und Flugblätter, Annoncen, Schilder und Plakate verwendet. Darin analysiert er den Straßenraum und, ähnlich der Street Art von heute, das Schreiben in der Stadt: „In the city writing turns graphic."

Roland Maurmair übersetzt menschliche Eigenschaften in seine Tierzeichnungen, kombiniert Bilder und öffentliche Räume, Objekte und Schrift, um Freiheitsdenken und Radikalität experimentell auszureizen. Die einzelnen Komponenten lässt er dabei jeweils ihrer eigenen, subversiven und höchst ironischen Logik folgen. Er steht damit in der Tradition der frühen Avantgardisten ebenso wie in jener der Street Art, anknüpfend an jene Brechungen und Forderungen, die schon Banksy formuliert hat: „A lot of people never use their initiative becaue no-one told them to!"[3]

---

2   Leslie, Esther: Hollywood Flatlands. Animation, Critical Theory and the Avant-Garde, London/New York 2004, S. 57
3   Banksy: Wall and Piece, London 2007, S. 21

12 V

Subversive Codes

Tereza Kotyk

Doesn't subversion ideally consist of rewriting codes instead of destroying them?
Roland Barthes

Roland Barthes' quote stands for the activist work of the Communication Guerrilla, a creative strategy towards subversion that, like anarchism, situationism, earlier avant-garde movements and the hacker culture, creatively processes and parodies well-known texts, pictures and signs as a means of exposing: expectations are unmasked, every-day experiences unsettled by distortion, and the practiced obedience to authorities is revealed.

In his graphic works, Roland Maurmair's primary focus is on the study of coded behaviour and systems. He uses techniques similar to those of the Communication Guerrilla: He waits in ambush as an artist, irritates expectations and creates confusion by removing familiar expressions and pictures from their usual context and placing them in a new one. To achieve this he does not remain attached to one medium but, starting with the drawing, adds installation elements or photographic works and combines mixed techniques such as potato print, coffee painting and stencil spraying.

With *Nest* (2006), Roland Maurmair created a graphic piece of work in the Kaufhaus Tyrol department store in Innsbruck that spread beyond the boundaries of paper with drawings being moved by rats over walls, cardboard boxes, crates, bags and the floor. In addition, a small engine in a plastic bag labelled with the instruction "Defendi la Natura" caused the paper to rustle. "Defend nature" is a call for initiative, whose intention however is contrasted by the rats: The rats symbolize an illusory world that is being gnawed at until eventually it is hollow and collapses. The rats were symbolically gnawing at the house, which was temporarily empty for renovation works, thus triggering a revolution from below in this hostile environment. Rats as resistance fighters just before the final collapse of a house that, being the most modern department store in western Austria at the time, was claimed as Aryan property by the Nazis in the Second World War.

The Africans are coming! (2005), is another piece of work where Maurmair installed reproductions of his screen print with the same title in the public space. The original, colourful and eye-catching screen print shows "African" men, women and children with suitcases who are travelling somewhere, looking for the right 'arrival'. This screen print inspires associations with words like migration, hope, family and displacement. In the past few years, some Austrian newspapers have been prejudging migrants, mostly Africans, and feeding prejudices against these ethnic groups, which have blossomed and bloomed in a rather unfriendly and racist atmosphere in Austria – described by Alois Brandstetter in his text "My first negro": The inheritance of old Hegelian thinking, which tries to prove the alien and animal-like character of the negro and whose prejudices we have incorporated in our thinking.[1] Maurmair produced small stickers of the original screen print, which can be seen in the public space in Innsbruck, Munich, Vienna, Torino, Berlin, Amsterdam and Barcelona. In this way, the screen print became part of a whole that formed a statement connecting these streets and cities with each other, the campaign in total representing a radical rejection of any form of racism. Racial prejudice is postulated in an eye-catching way; and Maurmair responds by employing the same means.

Contempt and hatred of the 'alien and animal-like' human being are contrasted by the general love of animals. Therefore, Maurmair not only uses stereotypical images of our human prejudices but also pictures and cartoons of animals: Maya the bee, Micky Mouse, goats, koala bears, pandas, turtles, snakes, centipedes, pigs, rabbits, ducks, armadillos, rats, cows, giraffes etc. all form subjects of his graphic works. His animals are assigned human traits, altered and attributed some ironic shift. They have personal, social and philosophical problems, fall in love or suffer from broken hearts – such as the armadillo that is obsessed with appearances and falls in love with a hand grenade (*Untitled*, 2006; see: *Me Jane, You Tarzan*, 2008).

---

1   Zaunschirm, Thomas: Das Tier im Menschen – was sind Taubstumme und Neger? (The animal in us – what are deaf mutes and Negroes?) in: Kunstforum International, Im Zoo der Kunst II (International Arts Forum: At the zoo of arts II), volume 175, Ruppichteroth April – May 2005, p. 71 et seq.

They are live with electricity or near death, face political and seemingly unsolvable problems (*Lately in Ramallah*, 2004). The image of the rabbit keeps reappearing: in these works, the rabbit mostly fights with his hero, the media-charged Duracell rabbit (*His Masters Voice*, 2009; *Natural Amplifier*, 2007; *Blind Date III*, 2006; *Blind Date II*, 2005) or becomes part of some performing action in the public space (*Rabbitism*, 2007).

In his graphic print series *Childhood Heroes*, the artist, inspired by every-day situations, the media and pictures of his own childhood, satirically portrays the tragic moments, adopting the idea of the tragic hero. Maurmair also refers to the aphorisms that guide us through every-day life and are supposed to give our lives meaning. The German saying *When you think there is no way forward a light will suddenly turn on somewhere* (2009) is the title of one of Maurmair's works showing Thumper, the rabbit in Disney's Bambi tale, who is setting Bambi's tail on fire behind his back. *When I'm older I wanna be an education budget* (2010) is another piece of work showing a happy Pumuckl – who is lying in his hammock and dreaming about the future, adding 0 + 1 = 2 – while *Free your ass, your mind will follow* (2009) depicts Winnie-the-Pooh who is breaking wind to help him lift his mood.

This form of humoristic shift contains messages on various levels: on the subject level containing an instruction (speech bubble) on the one hand, and on the definition level in the title (script) on the other. Maurmair's humanlike animal figures approach our existence very closely – in their vulnerability and sensitivity, in their exposedness, confusion and anger, in their longings, illusionary dreaming and hopeful plans for the future.

The animal is a metaphoric and symbolic detour to reach man. The "rats" mentioned above, in particular, and their subversive strategy to occupy, in a guerrilla-like manner, the street and the city as their habitat are a symbol of resistance. Their depiction is a continuation of the political statement in the critical area between 'high culture' and 'mass culture' (*Bienvenido, negrito!*, 2006).

Walter Benjamin already recognized the revolutionary character of this kind of combination of lines, drawing and humour as a subversive means to reverse coded behaviour.[2] In 1928 he published the book One Way Street, which was written in 'street code' using leaflets, advertisements, signs and posters. In this book he analyzes the street as a space of its own and, like today's Street Art, writing in the city, "In the city writing turns graphic."

Roland Maurmair translates human traits into his animal drawings, combining pictures and public space, objects and script, to experimentally exhaust liberal thinking and radicalism. In his works, each component follows its own subversive and highly ironic logic. Thus, he continues the tradition established by both the early avant-gardists and Street Art, reviving the challenges and appeals formulated by artists such as Banksy, "A lot of people never use their initiative because no-one [has] told them to!"[3]

2   Leslie, Esther: Hollywood Flatlands. Animation, Critical Theory and the Avant-Garde, London/New York 2004, p. 57
3   Banksy: Wall and Piece, London 2007, p. 21

free your

Pinocchio on World Tour

Ein kurzer Trip durch Raum und Zeit | a short trip through space and time

170 · braun · keine

11. PERSONSBESCHREIBUNG/SIGNALEMENT/DESCRIPTION OF BEARER

Größe
Taille
Height
170 cm

Farbe der Augen
Couleur des yeux
Colour of eyes
BRAUN

12. Besondere Kennzeichen
Signes particuliers/Distinguishing marks
KEINE

13. Unterschrift des Paßinhabers
Signature du titulaire/Holder's signature

14. Kinder/Enfants/Children

Name (1) und Vorname (2) Nom et prénom Surname and given name	Geburtsdatum (5) Date de naissance Date of birth	Geschlecht (3) Sexe Sex

Art/Type/Type P Kode/Code/Code AUT Paß-Nr/Passport N°/Passport No. J 0491907 3

1. Name/Nom/Surname
MAURMAIR

2. Vorname/Prénom/Given name
ROLAND HEINRICH

3. Geschlecht/Sexe/Sex
M

4. Staatsangehörigkeit/Nationalité/Nationality
ÖSTERREICH

5. Geburtsort/Lieu de naissance/Place of birth
INNSBRUCK

6. Geburtsdatum/Date de naissance/Date of birth
01.12.1975

9. Ausstellungsort/Lieu de délivrance/Place of issue
INNSBRUCK

10. Ausstellungsdatum/Date de délivrance/Date of issue
19.01.2004

Gültig bis/Date of expiry
18.01.2014

DIE BÜRGERMEISTERIN
DER STADT INNSBRUCK

DVR 0059331

GEBÜHR ENTRICHTET

P<AUTMAURMAIR<<ROLAND<HEINRICH<<<<<<<<<<<<<
J0491907<3AUT7512010M1401187<<<<<<<<<<<<<<8

Doppelspion mit Tarnkappe

Intervention 1999

Double agent with a magic hat

Intervention 1999

Hannibals Zug über die Alpen

Happening 2000

Hannibal's crossing of the Alps

Happening 2000

langweilig

Monochromalheur

Siebdruck | screen print 2004

Am Grab von Kasimir M.

Objekt 1999

At Kasimir M.'s grave

object 1999

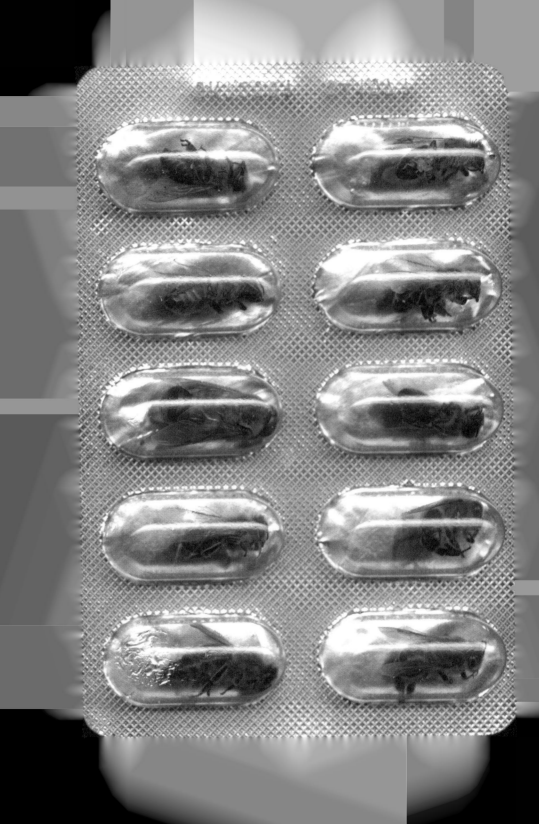

Sumsizäpfchen

Objekt 2000

Sumsi suppositories

object 2000

Original Tyrolean Sumsi suppositories
Content: 20 bees; Recommended daily allowance: one bee; 30 mg capsules;
A buzzzzzzzzzzzzzzzzzzzzzing sensation for him and her; Keep out of reach of children!

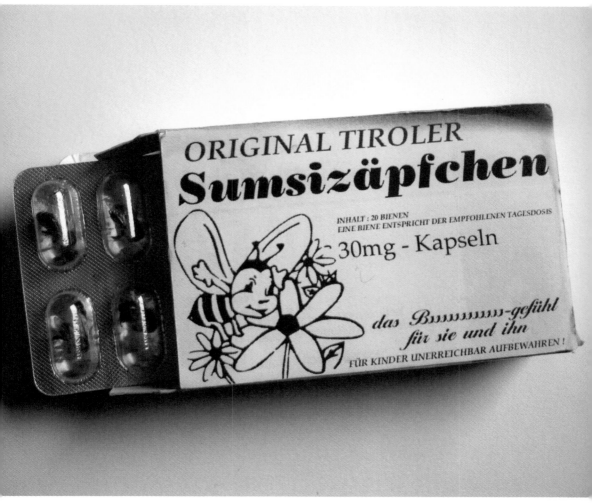

Fuck, it's raining!

Mischtechnik | mixed technique 2005

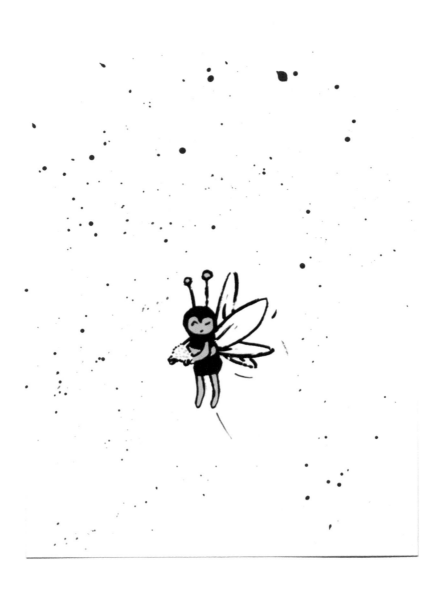

Raindrums

Installation | installation „Park of the Future", Amsterdam 2000

Saigon ultra

Objekt | object 2001

next · rotate · left right · down

The Never Miss a Mango-Tour

Composings, Vietnam/Austria 2004

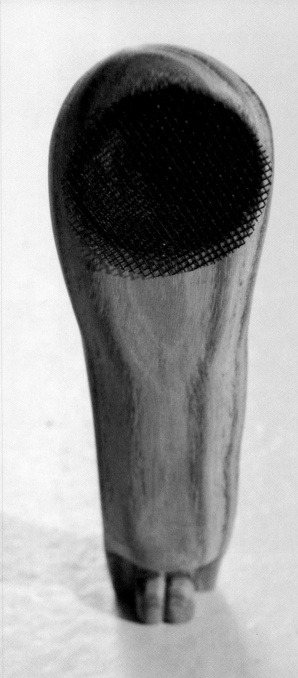

Burqababes

Objekt, Zeichung | object, drawing 2009/2010

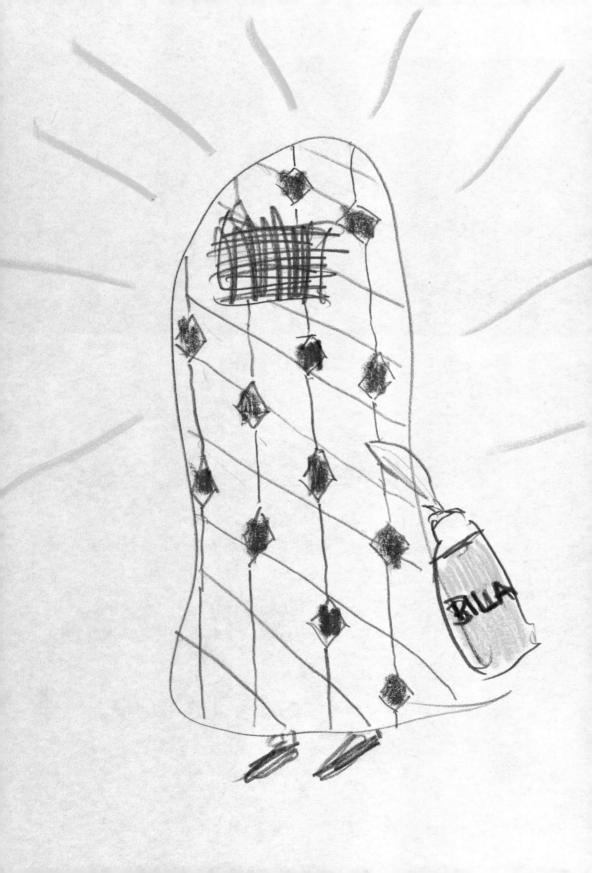

Transparenz des Bösen

oder **Maya und ihre Freunde halb zu Gast bei der halben Familie Gott**

Mischtechnik 2005

Transparency of the evil

or **Half of Maya and her friends visiting half the God family**

mixed technique 2005

Schlechter Empfang

Photo 2004

---

bad reception

photograph 2004

Camel [2]

Objekt | object 1996

Bluesbrüder

Composing 1998

12 monkeys

Siebdruck | screen print 2006

Jesus fue un terrorista

Siebdruck | screen print 2007

The legendary Piepshow

Multiple 2004

Vogelnest, Audiobox, CD-Walkman, CD mit künstlichen Piepsounds,
Bauanleitung, Siebdruck

Bird's nest, audio box, portable CD player, CD with artificial chirping sounds, construction manual,
screen print

Manticor

Objekt | object 2010

Ich wollt, ich wär ein Maulwurf

Objekt 2010

I wanna be a mole

object 2010

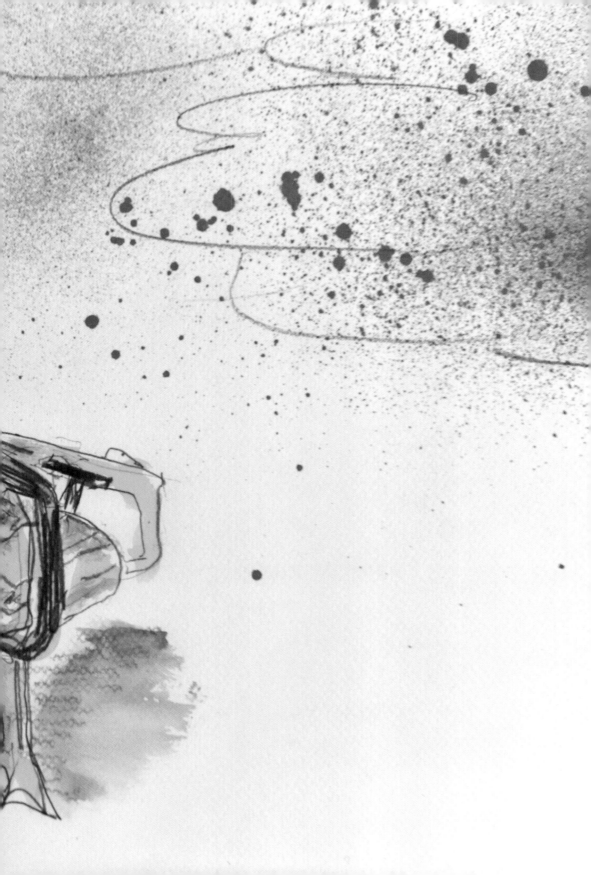

Herde – Rudel – Schwarm

Herde – Rudel – Schwarm

Herden, Rudel und auch Schwärme sind Tier-Aggregationen, deren Gemeinsamkeit unter anderem in der Synchronizität ihres Verhaltens ersichtlich wird.[1] Interessant ist, dass diese Gruppenbildungen vorrangig dazu dienen, das Überleben bzw. den Lebensstandard zu sichern. Ausschlaggebend ist also primär die ökonomische Effizienz. Während bei einem Rudel und bei Herden Familienzugehörigkeit und Rangordnung die entscheidenden Faktoren sind (vgl. Wolfsrudel oder Kuhherde), gelten bei Schwärmen einfache mathematische Prinzipien, die diese zu einem so genannten „Superorganismus" werden lassen. Bei diesem existiert keine zentrale Steuerung, was wiederum eine gewisse Kommunikationsfähigkeit der einzelnen Tiere miteinander beweist.[2] Diesem Phänomen kollektiver Intelligenz gilt mein Hauptaugenmerk.

Durch Beobachtung und Imitation der Natur hat der Mensch es scheinbar geschafft, sich über diese Natur zu stellen, eine Ordnung in ihr auszumachen und diese gezielt zu instrumentalisieren. Heutzutage lässt sich Schwarmverhalten in Computermodellen simulieren, die dabei gewonnenen Ergebnisse dienen zum Beispiel der Optimierung der Verkehrsregulierung auf unseren Autobahnen. Auf verheerende Weise hingegen entfaltet sich die Nachahmung des Schwarmverhaltens, wenn, wie beispielsweise im militärischen Kontext, unbemannte Flugzeuge als Drohnenschwarm auf ein Ziel gesteuert werden.

Indem der Mensch sich durch Nachahmung seiner „nächsten Verwandten"[3] behauptet, vergleicht er sich mit ihnen. Insekten werden als „Völker" oder „Kolonien" definiert, ja, man gesteht ihnen sogar zu, ganze „Staaten" zu bilden; wie umgekehrt der Mensch oft als „Herdenwesen" bezeichnet wird.[4] Am Tier sich ein Beispiel zu nehmen, sein Verhalten zu beobachten, es nachzuahmen und zu optimieren hat eine jahrtausendealte Tradition und macht vielleicht sogar zu einem Gutteil das Menschsein aus. Hat der Mensch in früheren Zeiten in Gruppen gejagt, so strebt er heute nach wie vor danach, sich mit seinesgleichen zusammenzutun, sich in Gruppen zu organisieren, um seine (sublimierten) Bedürfnisse zu stillen. Nicht zuletzt dadurch zeigt sich die enge verwandtschaftliche Beziehung zwischen Tier und Mensch, die, in verschiedenen Ausprägungen, sich durch das gesamte Projekt zieht.

Abb. rechts: *Bumblebee Kavallerie* primitives Medienobjekt (Überraschungseier, Türsummer, Kabel, Motor, Draht)
Fig. right: *Bumblebee Cavalry* primitive media object (Kinder Surprise egg, buzzer, wire, cable, engine)
Ortner2, Vienna 2010

---

1   „Schulen, Schwärme und Herden führen uns eindrucksvolle Beispiele für das koordinierte Verhalten einzelner Tiere in einem größeren Ganzen vor Augen. Tatsächlich finden wir solche Organisations- und Koordinationsmuster in allen Arten von tierischen Gesellschaften, denn sie liegen in der Natur solcher Verbände. Sie bilden den Kontext oder Rahmen für die Reaktionen und Beziehungen innerhalb einer Tiergesellschaft." (Vgl. Sheldrake, Rupert: Das Gedächtnis der Natur. Bern/München/Wien 2002, S. 289)
2   Laut Maturana und Varela kann das gegenseitige Auslösen von koordinierten Verhaltensweisen unter den Mitgliedern einer sozialen Einheit als Kommunikation verstanden werden. Vgl. Maturana, Humberto; Varela, Francisco (Hg.): Der Baum der Erkenntnis. Die biologischen Wurzeln des menschlichen Erkennens. Bern/München/Wien 1987, S. 210f.
3   Vgl. Dawkins, Richard: Geschichten vom Ursprung des Lebens. Eine Zeitreise auf Darwins Spuren. Berlin 2008
4   Vgl. Rousseau, Jean-Jacques: Der Gesellschaftsvertrag oder Die Grundsätze des Staatsrechtes. Frankfurt/Main 2000, S. 14

Thunfisch
Thunfisch
Thunfisch
Thunfisch
Wasser
Kochsalz
Zutaten: Thunfisch
e80g Wasser
Kochsalz
Zutaten: Thunfisch
e80g
Thunfisch
Wasser
Kochsalz

Herds – Packs – Flocks

Herds, packs and flocks are aggregations of animals, whose commonality is proved, among other things, by the synchronicity of their behaviour.[1] It is interesting that these group formations are primarily intended to ensure survival as well as efficient movements and behaviour of each group member. . In packs and herds family membership and rank orders are relevant factors (for example in a pack of wolves or a herd of cows) whereas in flocks, schools and swarms, mathematical principles are predominant, thus creating a super-organism. There is no central navigation system, which proves a certain ability of these animals to communicate with each other.[2] My main focus is on this collective intelligence.

By observing and imitating nature, man has apparently managed to place himself on a superior level, detect a certain order in the latter and instrumentalize it according to his needs. Nowadays flock simulations in computer models, for example, help to optimise traffic on our motorways. However, the imitation of flock behaviour has disastrous consequences when applied on a military level in the form of unmanned aircraft systems called "drones", which are used to perform attack missions on a certain target.

To the same extent that man stands up to its "closest relatives"[3] by imitation, he compares himself to them: insects are defined as states, populations or colonies, and people can equally be described as herds[4]. Following the animals' example, observing their behaviour, imitating and optimizing it has been a tradition for thousands of years, and may have influenced human behaviour on a large scale. In former times man used to hunt in groups; today he continues to long for the company of others, organising himself in groups in order to fulfil his (sublimated) needs. This, among other things, demonstrates the close (family) relationship between man and animal, which is a main element of the entire project.

---

1 „Schools, swarms and herds are all impressive examples of coordinated behaviour of individual animals in a larger group. As a matter of fact, we find such patterns of organization and coordination in all kinds of animal communities since they are typical of such associations. These patterns form the context or framework for the reactions and relationships within an animal community." (Cf. Sheldrake, Rupert: The Memory of Nature. Bern/Munich/Vienna 2002, p. 289)

2 According to Maturana and Varela, the act of triggering coordinated behaviour among the members of a social unit can be regarded as communication. Cf. Maturana, Humberto; Varela, Francisco (ed.): The Tree of Knowledge. The biological Roots of human cognition. Bern/Munich/Vienna 1987, p. 210 et seq.

3 Cf. Dawkins, Richard: Stories of the Origin of Life. A journey through time tracing Darwin's Path. Berlin 2008

4 Cf. Rousseau, Jean-Jacques: The Social Contract or Principles of Political Right. Frankfurt/Main 2000, p. 14.

Audiovisuelle Spannungen

Inge Hinterwaldner über Roland Maurmairs installative Arbeiten.

Die installativen Arbeiten Roland Maurmairs sind ein Appell an verschiedene Sinne. Der Künstler entwickelte im Laufe seines Schaffens eine besondere, halb-intuitive Sensibilität, intensiv auf Umwelteindrücke einzugehen und diese in seinen Werken zu verarbeiten. Inspiration schöpft er gleichermaßen aus Erlebnissen in den Bergen und aus künstlichen Pseudo-Naturwelten wie städtischen Parkanlagen. Die bildnerischen Umsetzungen weisen dabei häufig erkennbare figurative Komponenten auf. Eine simple Zuordnung oder eindeutige Gegenstandsidentifikation erlaubt dies jedoch nicht. Denn optische, akustische und haptische Eindrücke verschränken sich in seinen Arbeiten nicht selten auf eine Weise, die jene Betrachter ins Grübeln bringt, welche die Werke vor allem nach Kohärenz und Kompatibilität mit der Realität befragen. Ohne dass man der Idee anhängen müsste, Kunst habe einen Ausschnitt der Welt konzise abzubilden, will man in aller Regel doch verstehen, worin diese Dissonanz besteht. Es handelt sich nicht um etwas Mysteriöses; es entsteht auch nicht der Eindruck, etwas gehe hier nicht mit rechten Dingen zu. Vielmehr scheint hier etwas *anders* zu funktionieren als auf den ersten Blick angenommen. Die Alltagserfahrung des Betrachters bildet den Ausgangspunkt für dessen Beurteilung des Unterbreiteten *als Alternative*.

Ein Klärung versprechender Weg tut sich auf, sobald man sich formal oder wahrnehmungsästhetisch motivierte Fragen stellt: Wie kann etwa das Akustische im Verbund mit dem Visuellen dem Betrachter ein Sinnesangebot unterbreiten, das dieser erst in einem zweiten Schritt über eigene Erinnerungen und Rekonstruktionen der Konsistenz überführen kann? Der Beobachter muss Einiges investieren, damit das hintergründig Transformierte sich schließlich als Schlüssiges zu erkennen gibt. Wie ist die Verschiebung und Interaktion der Sinnesmodalitäten in den einzelnen Werken beschreibbar? Inwiefern folgt daraus eine aussagekräftige Spaltung und Spannung? Welche Strategie steckt hinter dieser künstlerischen Neuordnung der Eindrücke anhand zunächst bekannt erscheinender Phänomene? Diese und ähnliche Fragen provoziert eine eingehendere Auseinandersetzung mit Maurmairs Installationen.

Verdunkeln durch Öffnen. Otto E. Rössler ist Chaosforscher und Endophysiker. Er geht davon aus, dass man in der Physik neben dem Untersuchungsobjekt auch das forschende Gehirn des Wissenschafters mit zu berücksichtigen hat, dem nur eine Schnittstelle zur Welt zur Verfügung steht.[1] Auf Rösslers Theorie nimmt Maurmair in seiner Klanginstallation *Sind wir nicht alle ein bisschen endo?* (2000) Bezug. Diese Arbeit wurde in einem fensterlosen Raum realisiert, in dem sechs einzelne Audioboxen von der Decke hängen. Diese sind von länglichen, hellen Filzcocoons umhüllt. Nicht erst seit Joseph Beuys steht Filz für Geborgenheit und Wärme. In diesem Fall sollen die Cocoons den intimen Privatgesprächen Schutz bieten, die aus den Lautsprechern zu vernehmen sind. Nichtsdestotrotz dringen gedämpft Geräusche durch die weiche Ummantelung, sodass Inhalte der Privatsphäre in die Öffentlichkeit durchsickern. In Ermangelung entsprechender Begrifflichkeiten für den akustischen Bereich, könnte man sagen, dass man als Besucher der Installation zwar nicht den freien 'auditiven Zublick' hat, aber zumindest das Äquivalent eines 'auditiven Gucklochs'.

---

1   Vgl. Rössler, Otto E.: Endophysik, die Welt des inneren Beobachters, Merve: Berlin 1992. Rössler, Otto E.: Vom Chaos, der virtuellen Realität und der Endophysik, 1996, in: Telepolis, in: http://www.heise.de/tp/r4/ artikel/5/5004/1.html (1.2.2011).

Man wird zwangsläufig zum Gesprächsvoyeur, sobald man den Raum betritt. Ein Ausweg aus der unfreiwilligen Einbezogenheit wird aber auch in Aussicht gestellt. An einer Wand ist ein Kästchen mit der Aufschrift "Exit" befestigt, ein Austreten aus der akustischen Sphäre scheint möglich. Folgerichtig materialisiert sich der Fluchtweg in Form entnehmbarer Ohrstöpsel. Verwendet man sie, legt man eine weitere Schutzschicht über die durch die halb durchlässige Filzumhüllung nur unzulänglich abgedichteten Gesprächsmitschnitte. Oder kapselt man eher sich selbst von einer Außenwelt ab? Wo verlaufen die Grenzen zwischen den Bereichen, in denen man involviert (endo) ist und bei denen man sich ausklinken und so etwas wie eine Außenperspektive (exo) einnehmen kann? Verhalten sich der visuelle und der akustische Eindruck dabei analog oder verlaufen sie quer zueinander? Einen Hinweis darauf erhält man, sobald man das Schränkchen öffnet. Dann nämlich wird es von innen beleuchtet, ein Mechanismus, den man vom Kühlschrank kennt. Aber zugleich passiert das Unerwartete: Der Raum, in dem man sich befindet, verdunkelt sich. Nun verursacht die Bewegung des Öffnens generell niemals eine Verdunkelung. Dunkelheit kann nicht punktuell ausstrahlen, wie etwa das Licht. Die Alltagserfahrung wird gründlich umgestülpt, neue Zusammenhänge oder Kausalitäten werden denk- und erlebbar gemacht. Sowohl über den dumpf-abgeschotteten Ton als auch über die Verdunkelung entzieht sich das Vorhandene der Vernehm- bzw. der Wahrnehmbarkeit. Der Besucher ist dadurch stärker auf sich und auf die eigenen Sinneskapazitäten zurückgeworfen. "Exit" ist somit ein "Enter" im Sinne eines Ankommens bei sich selbst. Andererseits befindet man sich immer noch in der Welt, nur wird einem über die Deprivierung die Begrenztheit des eigenen Zugangs bewusst.

Unsichtbare Hindernisse hörbar. Die Audioinstallation *heavy-G-rain* (2009) ist auf den ersten Blick vergleichbar aufgebaut. Sie besteht aus einer Konstruktion mit dreißig Audioboxen, die einzeln an Kabeln befestigt auf unterschiedlichen Höhen von der Decke hängen. Hier gibt jeder Lautsprecher kurze Tonschnipsel (grains) aufprallender Regentropfen wieder. Linear fragmentierte Samples werden derart resynthetisiert, dass über die verteilten Lautsprecher im Raum eine komplexe, multidimensionale Erfahrung eines Gewitters vermittelt wird.

Nun hört man Regentropfen eigentlich nur bei deren Aufprall und nicht während ihres Falls. Folglich müsste man zur Plausibilisierung des Geräuschs annehmen, dass sich auf der jeweiligen Höhe der Lautsprecher Hindernisse befinden. Diese sind in der Installation jedoch de facto nicht gegeben, sondern müssen gedanklich ergänzt werden. Der Besucher kann zudem zwischen den einzelnen, mehr oder minder auf Kopfhöhe positionierten Lautsprechern umhergehen, ohne jedoch mit den dort anzunehmenden Gegenständen zu interferieren. Er kann sich ganz dicht an die Stelle des gehörten Auftreffens des Tropfens begeben, so als hätte er sein Ohr einer unteren Begrenzung angenähert. Eine derartige Erfahrung könnte im wirklichen Leben am ehesten in einem Laubwald gemacht werden, wo sich die einzelnen Blätter als filigrane Flächen den fallenden Wassertröpfchen in den Weg stellen. Akustisch bildet sich auf diese Weise eine Klangwolke, optisch nicht. Im Visuellen lassen sich die vertikal herabhängenden Kabel mit dem letzten Stück Wegstrecke der fallenden Tropfen assoziieren. Diese angedeuteten Trajektorien sind wie 'eingefroren' dauerhaft präsent, während der Regenfall akustisch variiert und das kollektive Tröpfeln sich als ein ständig veränderndes Rauschen darbietet. Die von oben kommenden Trajektorien der Tropfen bildeten damit das 'Negativ' einer zu imaginierenden Waldlandschaft, wobei die Position der Lautsprecher punktuell die Grenze zwischen freiem Fall und Aufprallstelle anzeigen. Ist der Luftraum nur vereinzelt von den Kabelsträngen durchzogen, ist der akustische Raum ungleich 'voller'.

Auch bei der Installation *Separatistenkongress* (2008), in der kleine, farbige Plastikbälle im Raum mit dünnen Nylonfäden an der Decke montiert und dann mit einem Ventilator in Bewegung versetzt werden, geht es um eine luftige Bestückung des Innenraumvolumens. Ähnlich verfährt die Arbeit *Shiny Ugly Galaxy* (2007), bei welcher der Künstler weiß gefärbte Föhrenzapfen dreidimensional räumlich verteilt auf eine Drahtkonstruktion aufhängt, welche wiederum mit den für New Orle-

ans ortspezifischen bunten 'Mardi Gras'-Ketten behangen wurde. In diesen letzten beiden Fällen der Raumbestückung gibt es auch jeweils ein kontrastierendes starres Zentrum, jedoch kreiert der Künstler hier keine Dissoziation – und damit Spannung – zwischen akustischem und optischem Phänomen. Wann immer Ton und Strom im Spiel sind, treten bei Maurmair bewusst nicht kaschierte Kabelstränge in Erscheinung, etwa bei der massiv verkabelten Bienengesellschaft *Bumblebee-Kavallerie* (2010). Diese besteht aus Plastikbehältern von Kinderüberraschungseiern, kommuniziert mittels Türsummern und wird durch eine rotierende Drahtkonstruktion schwerfällig ausgelenkt.

Richtungsumkehrung. Die Audioplastik *Dandelion* (2006) kennzeichnet sich durch Stielaugen oder Greifärmchen, die von einem bauchigen Kugelvolumen ausgehen. Diese organisch und zugleich dafür doch zu perfekt geometrisch angeordneten Ausbuchtungen erweisen sich jedoch weder als Seh- noch als Tastorgane, sondern sind kleine Sendestationen für akustische Signale. Während beim Regen eine Emissionsrichtung (senkrecht nach unten) vorherrscht, strahlen die 64 Mini-Audioboxen hier von einem Zentrum in alle Richtungen aus. Zu hören ist das Fauchen des Windes und ein menschliches Pusten, Blasen oder Pfeifen. Spätestens sobald man diese akustischen Versatzstücke, denen ein künstlicher oder natürlicher Luftzug gemein ist, vernommen hat, nehmen auch die Assoziationen mit der Botanik überhand. Die Verbindung mit einer Pusteblume gelingt sowohl durch den Titel der Arbeit ("Dandelion" bedeutet im Deutschen Löwenzahn),

wie auch durch die optische Erscheinung der ansprechenden und vornehmlich in weiß gehaltenen Plastik. Nicht immer bedient sich der Künstler bei seinen Klangobjekten einer solchen glatten Verkleidung. Wenn bei *Dandelion* nur das Audio-Interface und das technische Setting offen und 'roh' stehenbleiben, setzt Maurmair in anderen Arbeiten den „Lowtech-Charme" oft expliziter in Szene. Doch zurück zu *Dandelion* und den damit evozierten Vorstellungen: Ein feinhaarig aufgeplusterter Löwenzahn in der Samenreife und der Impuls, die Samen mit ihren Flugschirmen durch das Anhauchen in die Welt hinauszuschicken,

Abb. 1a-b/Fig. 1a-b

bilden in vielen Kindheitserinnerungen eine untrennbare Einheit. Die französischen Künstler Edmond Couchot und Michel Bret reanimierten diese Erfahrung in ihrer frühen interaktiven Computerarbeit "Pissenlit" (1990; siehe Abb. 1a-b). Die Besucher konnten in ein Interface hineinblasen, um dann das rechnergenerierte Davonfliegen der einzelnen Samen auf dem Bildschirm zu beobachten. Konkret bewerkstelligte man hier also über eine technische Schnittstelle die Übertragung eines realen Windstoßes in die Computerszenerie, was dort verblüffenderweise die in der Sache erwartbaren Veränderungen auslöste. Im Gegensatz dazu ist in Maurmairs Arbeit die Pflanze 'hardwaremäßig' realisiert und kann eine vergleichbare Flexibilität wie in der Computergrafik kaum aufweisen. Aber auch in anderer Hinsicht besteht ein grundlegender Unterschied: Es herrscht eigentlich Windstille, weil ein Luftzug weder installativ realisiert ist, noch die Besucher angehalten werden, einen solchen zu erzeugen. Nun wird das Paradox der Arbeit deutlich: Hier erfährt nicht die Blütenplastik die Windstöße; im Gegenteil, durch eine Richtungsumkehrung ist sie es, die faucht, haucht, hustet und prustet. Bei *Dandelion* hört man das Pusten, man sieht es aber nicht und auch nicht die Auswirkungen. Die Audioplastik endet nicht an der ertastbaren Oberfläche, sondern greift akustisch in den Raum ein. Da die aufgezeichneten Geräusche zwischen den verschiedenen Lautsprechern wechseln, werden sie fluktuierend wahrgenommen. Die wandernden Signale bilden sozusagen eine akustische Aura um den Kern der Plastik. Sie haben das Ohr des Besuchers und seine Vorstellungskraft zum Ziel. Was wohl soll angetrieben, weggeschoben oder abgekühlt werden? Durch die pustende Cyberblume fühlt man sich mal angelockt, mal eher verscheucht.

Über das Visuelle zum Akustischen und umgekehrt. Über die Lautsprecher wird die Luft unbemerkt in Schwingung versetzt, auch wenn man diesen Vorgang ohne verstärkende Mechanismen nicht wahrnehmen kann. Bei entsprechender Lautstärke genügt es, den eigenen (Resonanz-)Körper zu beobachten, um sich dessen zu vergewissern. Eine andere Möglichkeit besteht darin, eine feine Membran zu beschallen, um dieses Phänomen dadurch in den sichtbaren Bereich zu verschieben. Dies realisiert Maurmair in seiner interaktiven Arbeit *Bärlappfeldgenerator* (2005). Damit knüpft er an eine Tendenz der Medienkunst an, oft quer zu den wissenschaftlich etablierten Verfahren und Epistemiken über Visualisierungstechniken und Sonifikationen Dispositive zu erproben, um dadurch das Erfahrungsspektrum zu erweitern. Beim *Bärlappfeldgenerator* stellt Maurmair dem Publikum zwei von der Decke hängende Mikro-

Bärlappfeldgenerator

phone zur Verfügung. In unmittelbarer Nähe befindet sich am Boden eine runde Membran, die über eine Unterkonstruktion mit mehreren Lautsprechern gespannt wurde, um von dieser akustische Impulse zu empfangen. Die eingespielten Sinusfrequenzen werden unterbrochen, sobald ein Besucher in das Mikrophon spricht oder singt. Entsprechend des Audiosignals gerät die gespannte Folie auf unterschiedliche Weise in Wallung. Schon der Naturforscher Ernst Florens Friedrich Chladni (1756–1827) verwendete staubartige Partikel, um Ton in Raumdimensionen zu übersetzen:[2] Mit Hilfe eines Geigenbogens versetzte er bestreute Metallplatten mechanisch in Schwingung (Abb. 2). Auf Chladnis Erkenntnisse aufbauend, ließ der US-amerikanische HNO-Arzt und Stimmtherapeut Henry Holbrook Curtis (1856–1920) professionelle Sänger in ein eigens entwickeltes Gerät, den Tonographen, singen, mit dem es ihm gelang, Klangfiguren photografisch zu fixieren. Identische Tonhöhen (also identische Schwingungen) riefen zwar immer dieselben typischen Figuren hervor, diese aber erfuhren durch den individuellen Ausdruck vielfältige Modifikationen, weswegen der Tonograph in Folge auch für Gesangsübungen verwendet wurde.

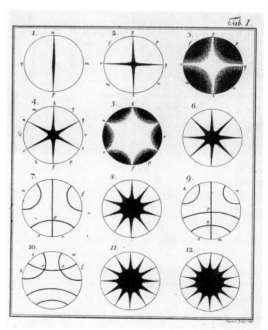

Abb .2/Fig. 2

2   Vgl. Chladni, Ernst F. F.: Entdeckungen über die Theorie des Klangs, Weidmanns Erben & Reich: Leipzig 1787. Chladni, Ernst F. F.: Die Akustik, Breitkopf und Haertel: Leipzig 1802. Mag man manchen Theorien glauben, so sind die durch Chladni berühmt gewordenen Klangfiguren schon im Mittelalter als Visualisierung von Musik genutzt worden, etwa in der Rosslyn Chapel (1440–1480). Vgl. Mitchell, Thomas James: Rosslyn Chapel. The Music of the Cubes, Diversions Books, 2006. Kritisch dazu: o.A.: Rosslyn Chapel – ,Music of the Cubes' (or should that be ,Rubes'?), in: The BS Historian. Sceptical Commentary on Pseudohystory and the Paranormal, Februar 2008, in: http://bshistorian.wordpress.com/2007/05/28/rosslyn-chapel-music-of-the-rubes/ (12.1.2011).

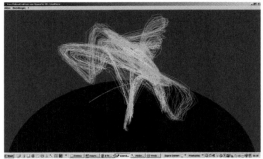

Was mit einer Möglichkeit für Gesangsstudenten, die Stimmbildung mittels des visuellen Biofeedbacks zu perfektionieren, begann, findet auch heute Fortsetzungen – beispielsweise in Attraktorrekonstruktionen der Stimme, wie sie 2001 am ZKM (Zentrum für Kunst und Medientechnologie in Karlsruhe) durch Hans H. Diebner und Sebastian Fischer unternommen wurden (Abb. 3a-b).

Variiert man die Stimme, erhält man verschiedene Muster (Attraktorformen) in der rein digitalen Phasenraumdarstellung.

Abb. 3a/Fig. 3a

Über das Mikrophon und den daran gekoppelten Lautsprecher als Frequenzgenerator gelang Maurmair beim *Bärlappfeldgenerator* eine Verbindung zwischen analoger und elektronischer Domäne. Der Künstler legte zur Verstärkung des Effekts mikroskopisch kleine Bärlappsporen auf die Membran, die sich je nach Tonlage charakteristisch verteilen, weil die Membran an verschiedenen Stellen unterschiedlich vibriert.[3] Mit ein und demselben Setting kann man je nach Interesse auf verschiedene Aspekte abzielen – und je nachdem ändert sich der Stellenwert der verwendeten Körnchen:

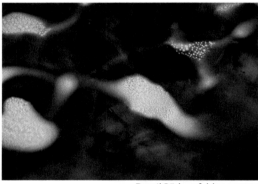

Sie können zum einen als Tracermaterial für die aus der gesprochenen Sprache entnommenen und umgesetzten Schwingungen gesehen werden. Zum anderen kann die Stimme bzw. der Ton als Trigger für die Musterformationen fungieren. In letzterem Fall tritt stärker das biologische Material in den Blick, das man in Maurmairs Anordnung in einer vergrößerten Petrischale vor sich hat. Beide Male handelt es sich um eine Art Versuchsanordnung, einmal mit Fokus auf das Akustische, einmal auf die (optische) Reaktion des Substrats. Beim *Bärlappfeldgenerator* ist es am Besucher, für sich zu entscheiden, ob er stärker seine Stimme

Detail Bärlappfeldgenerator

durch das Muster affizieren lässt und gezielt eine Formation nachahmt – oder umgekehrt das Muster durch die Stimme formt und eine Variationsbreite im visuellen Ergebnis anstrebt.

In seinen Installationen realisiert Maurmair Situationen, die sich von den alltäglichen Seh- und Hörgewohnheiten abheben, indem sie Verschiebungen aufweisen. Diese können als unerwartete kausale Verkettungen daherkommen oder eine Umgewichtung der beiden Sinnesmodalitäten bedeuten. Eine Diskrepanz zwischen aktiv und passiv (pusten – angepustet werden) oder zwischen Gesehenem und Gehörten trifft man genauso an wie die Möglichkeit, über eine visuelle Referenz eine akustische Formung herbeizuführen und umgekehrt. Auf diese Weise offeriert der Künstler seinem Publikum Sinnesangebote, die sich erst nach und nach erschließen und eine ungeahnte Vielschichtigkeit offenbaren.

---

3 An dieser Stelle sei kurz erwähnt, dass die winzigen Samen des Lykopodiums in der Physik in verschiedenen Bereichen eine erstaunliche Karriere hingelegt haben. In Wasser gemischt konnte der schottische Botaniker Robert Brown (1773–1858) 1827 mit Hilfe der hinreichend kohäsiven kleinen Körnchen temperaturabhängige Bewegungen der Flüssigkeitsmoleküle experimentell beobachten. Erst 1905 gelang Albert Einstein (1879–1955) und Marian von Smoluchowski (1872–1909) die mathematische Formulierung der so genannten Brownschen Molekularbewegung. Ab Ende des 19. Jahrhunderts benutzte der Zoologe Friedrich Ahlborn (1858–1937) die Sporen, um die nichtlineare Dynamik turbulenter Strömungen photografisch festhalten und analysieren zu können.

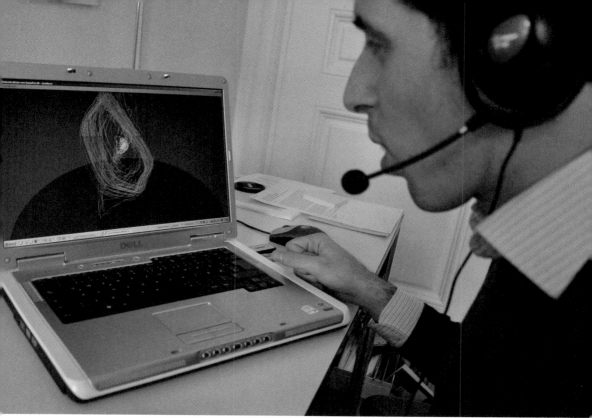

Abb. 3b/Fig. 3b

Abbildungen

Abb. 1a-b: Edmond Couchot und Michel Bret: Pissenlit, 1990. Screenshots, interaktive Computerinstallation.
Aus: Maria Zambrano: Graines dans mes poches, 2005, in: http://belcikowski.org/la_dormeuse/images2/couchot_
dandelion2.jpg (2.2.2011). Edmond Couchot, Michel Bret, 1998, in: http://www-inrev.univ-paris8.fr/extras/Michel-
Bret/cours/bret/travaux/presse/1998/BeauxArts_1998.htm (2.2.2011).

Abb. 2: Ernst Florens Friedrich Chladni: Klangfiguren auf einer runden Platte, 1787.
Aus: Ernst Florens Friedrich Chladni: Entdeckungen über die Theorie des Klanges. Mit elf Kupfertafeln, Weidmanns
Erben und Reich: Leipzig 1787, Tabelle 1.

Abb. 3a-b: Hans H. Diebner und Sebastian Fischer: LiveReco 2.1, 2001. Screenshot und Dokumentationsphoto der
interaktiven Computeranwendung.
Aus: LifeReco, in: http://fisch-im-netz.gmxhome.de/livereco.html (2.2.2011).

Audiovisual tensions

Inge Hinterwaldner on Roland Maurmair's installation works.

Roland Maurmair's works appeal to various senses. Over time, the artist has developed some special half-intuitive sensitivity to respond to external impressions with great intensity and process them in his works. He is also inspired by experiences in the mountains or artificial pseudo-natural environments such as urban parks. His visual works frequently contain recognizable figurative components. However, these do not allow for simple equations or conclusive identifications with certain objects since visual, acoustic and haptic impressions more often than not intertwine in such a way that leaves those puzzled who judge the works according to their coherence and compatibility with reality. Without necessarily clinging to the idea that art must be a concise representation of a segment of the world, we generally still want to understand this dissonance. There is nothing mysterious to it; nor do we get the impression that something is wrong. Things rather seem to work differently than we first assumed. Each observer's individual every-day experience forms the basis for his or her assessment of what has been offered as an alternative. Enlightenment dawns as soon as we start asking ourselves questions based on formal aspects or aesthetic perception: How can, for instance, a combination of acoustic and visual impressions provide the viewer with a sensory offer whose consistency he can only prove in a second step via his own memories and reconstructions. The viewer must invest quite a lot for the subtly transformed to finally reveal itself as a conclusive entity. How can the shift and interaction of sensory modalities in each work be described? How do they create meaningful rupture and tension? What is the strategy behind this creative rearrangement of impressions with the aid of phenomena that seem to be familiar at first sight? These and other similar questions provoke a desire to delve more deeply into Maurmair's installations.

Darkening by opening. Otto E. Roessler is a chaos theoretician and endophysicist. He believes that physics should take into account not only the object of research but also the brain of the researching scientist, who only has one interface to the world.[1] Maurmair refers to Roessler's theory in his sound installation *Aren't we all a little bit endo?* (2000). This work was realized in a window-less room with six separate audio boxes hanging from the ceiling. These were wrapped in longish light felt cocoons. Since long before Joseph Beuys, felt has been a symbol of emotional security and warmth. In this case, the cocoons are intended to protect the intimate private conversations coming from the loudspeakers. Despite their protection, muffled sounds can be heard through the soft cushioning so that parts of the privacy leak through. Given the lack of adequate terms for acoustic perceptions, visitors to the installation could be said to have, if not a free 'auditory view', at least the equivalent of an 'auditory peephole'. Upon entering the room, the visitor is automatically forced into the position of a conversation voyeur. However, a way out of this involuntary involvement is offered: There is a box labelled Exit on the wall, so that leaving the acoustic sphere appears to be an option. With earplugs placed there at the visitors' free disposal, it is perfectly logical that the Exit offers an escape route. Through the use of these earplugs another protective layer is wrapped around the snatches of conversation that are muted insufficiently by the semi-soundproof felt covers. Or are you rather shutting yourself out of the world around you? Where are the boundaries between the fields requiring active participation (endo) and those you can withdraw from in order to take an outward perspective (exo)? Are visual and acoustic impressions analogous to or disconnected from each other? The visitor gets a vague notion as soon as he uncloses the box: Upon opening, it is illuminated from within – a mechanism that we know from the fridge. And then the unexpected

---

1   Cf. Roessler, Otto E.: Endophysics, The World as an Interface, Merve: Berlin 1992. Roessler, Otto E.: Chaos, Virtual Reality and Endophysics, 1996, in: Telepolis, in: http://www.heise.de/tp/r4/artikel/5/5004/1.html (February 01, 2011).

happens: The surrounding room becomes dark. In our experience, the act of opening something is not related to the darkening of a room. Unlike light, darkness does not send beams. Every-day experience is turned upside down, and new connections and causalities become conceivable and tangible. Embedded by muffled sound and darkness, the room as a whole becomes inaudible and imperceptible. Therefore, the visitor is forced to rely more strongly on his own sensory skills. Exit therefore stands for Entrance to your own world. Even though we are still in the real world, the deprivation makes us aware of the limitations of our own access.

Invisible obstructions made audible. At first sight, the audio installation *heavy-G-rain* (2009) is constructed in a comparable way. It is made of a construction of 30 audio boxes, each of which is attached to the ceiling on cables, hanging down to different heights. Each loudspeaker emits grains of the sound of raindrops hitting the ground. In this way linear fragmented samples are re-synthesised so that a complex, multidimensional experience of a rainstorm is gained via the loudspeakers that are distributed across the room.

Now, as a matter of fact, you can only hear the raindrops hit an object rather than their actual fall. In order to make the sound more plausible, it would be logical to assume that there are barriers at the heights of the loudspeakers. However, no such obstacles actually exist in the installation; the visitor must add them by using his imagination. Besides, the visitor can walk around between the loudspeakers that are positioned more or less above eye level without interfering with the objects conjured up. He can step close to the spot where the raindrops can be heard, just as if his ear had reached a bottom limit. In real life, such an experience could most likely be made in a forest of broad-leaved trees, where the leaves form thin layers obstructing the path of the falling raindrops. A wave of sound is created acoustically but not visually. On the visual level, the cables hanging down vertically from the ceiling can be associated with the last part of the raindrops' path. These suggested trajectories are "frozen" into a permanent presence while the rainfall varies acoustically, its collective dripping forming a murmur that constantly changes. The trajectories of the raindrops can therefore be seen as the "negative" of an imaginary forest, the positions of the loudspeakers forming a punctual borderline between free fall and the site of impact. In comparison to the 'air-space', which is streaked by just a few cables here and there, the 'acoustic space' is by far more "occupied".

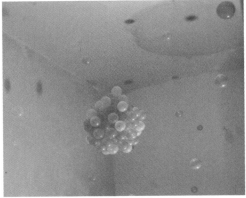

Separatists' Congress

The installation entitled *Separatists' Congress* (2008), which consists of small colourful plastic balls that are attached to the ceiling with thin nylon threads and set in motion by a fan, is also about lightly filling the volume of internal space. *Shiny Ugly Galaxy* (2007) is similar in that the artist three-dimensionally attaches pinecones that have been dyed white to a wire construction, which has been decorated with the colourful Mardi Gras necklaces that are typical of New Orleans. In these last two cases of three-dimensional art, each space also has a contrasting, i.e. rather inflexible centre, which, however, does not show any dissociation, or tension between the acoustic and visual phenomenon as a result. Whenever sound and electricity are involved, Maurmair quite intentionally uses unconcealed wiring, like for instance in the heavily wired *Bumblebee Cavalry* (2010). It is made of plastic Kinder Surprise eggs, communicates via the humming sound emitted by automatic door openers and is controlled in awkward movements by a rotating wire construction.

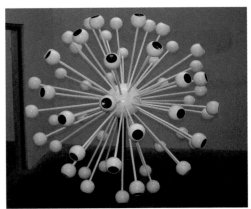

Dandelion

Reversal of directions. The audio-plastic construction *Dandelion* (2006) features telescope eyes/gripper arms protruding from a globular ball-shaped torso. The structure, which is reminiscent of an organic system, yet is arranged far too perfectly geometrically for an organic body, turns out to contain neither visual nor tactile organs but small transmitters for acoustic signals. While for the rain one (vertical) emission direction (from the ceiling to the ground) predominates, here 64 mini audio boxes emit their sound from one centre in all directions. You can hear the wind roar intermingled with human gasping, blowing or whistling. Once you have heard these movable pieces of sound, all of which represent some form of artificial or natural movement of air, associations with botany increasingly start to form. Not only is this piece of work associated with a blowball because of its title *Dandelion*, but also due to its attractive design mainly in white. The artist does not always use such a smooth 'jacket' for his sound objects. While in *Dandelion* only the audio interface and the technical setting remain open and 'raw', Maurmair highlights the 'low tech charm' of his installations more explicitly in other works. But let's return to *Dandelion* und the ideas it evokes: Many people's memories inextricably associate the seed head of white fluffy dandelions with an impulse to send out the parachute seeds by blowing them off into the world. The French artists Edmond Couchot and Michel Bret reanimated this experience in their early interactive computer work "Pissenlit" (1990; fig. 1a-b/p. 200). Visitors could blow into an interface and then watch the computer-generated dispersal of the seeds on the screen. To be more precise, a technical interface was used to transmit a real breath of wind into the computer scenery, which surprisingly triggered the changes expected after said action. In contrast, the plant in Maurmair's work was materialized on the 'hardware level'; therefore, its flexibility can hardly be compared to the computer graphics. And there is another fundamental difference on a different level: There is no wind really, as the installation is not designed to create any movement of air just as the visitors are not encouraged to provoke any such movement either.

Now the paradox of the installation becomes clear: It is not the plastic dandelion that is whipped by the wind, it is a reversal of directions where the flower itself blows, roars, howls and whistles. In *Dandelion* you can hear the moaning, yet you cannot see it or the impact it has. The audio-plastic construction does not end with the tangible surface but extends acoustically into space, fluctuating as the recorded sounds are emitted by alternate loudspeakers. The moving signals form an acoustic aura around the centre of the plastic installation. They are intended to reach the visitor's ear and his imagination. What is being blown, howled or roared at and why? The roaring, blowing and whistling cyber flower has both an alluring and a repellent effect at the same time.

From the visual to the acoustic and vice-versa. Unnoticed by our eyes and ears, loudspeakers cause the air to oscillate. However, this is a process we cannot perceive without amplifying mechanisms. With the volume turned up high enough, it is sufficient to observe our own (resonating) body to notice the oscillation. Another way to make the phenomenon visible is through the use of a fine membrane. This is what Maurmair does in his interactive work *Club Moss Field Generator* (2005). In this piece of work he incorporates the tendency of the media arts to try out dispositive methods by applying visualization techniques and sonification contrasting scientifically established techniques and knowledge in order to

Club Moss Field Generator

broaden the horizon of experience. The *Club Moss Field Generator* consists of two microphones hanging down from the ceiling. Directly underneath there is a round membrane on the floor that has been stretched over a construction of several loudspeakers so that the it receives acoustic impulses from this construction. The automatic sinus frequencies are interrupted as soon as a visitor speaks or sings into the microphone. Depending on the intensity of the audio signal, the foil starts to ripple in different ways. German physicist Ernst Florens Friedrich Chladni (1756–1827), who was dedicated to the research of nature, already used dust-like particles to translate sound into spatial dimensions:[2] He used a violin bow to mechanically cause metal plates covered with these particles to vibrate (fig.2/p. 201). Based on Chladni's findings, ENT physician and voice therapist Henry Holbrook Curtis (1856–1920) had professional singers sing into a specially designed machine, the tonograph, with which he managed to photographically depict patterns of sound. Identical pitches (i.e. identical vibrations) kept producing the same typical patterns, which, however, displayed a large variety of modifications as a result of each singer's individual expression. Subsequently the tonograph was also used for singing exercises.

---

2   Cf. Chladni, Ernst F.F.: Discoveries about the Theory of Sound, Weidmanns Erben & Reich: Leipzig 1787. Chladni, Ernst F.F.: Acoustics, Breitkopf und Haertel: Leipzig 1802. According to certain theories, the patterns of sound that have become famous because of Chladni were already used to visualize music in the Middle Ages, e.g. at the Rosslyn Chapel (1440–1480). Cf. Mitchell, Thomas James: Rosslyn Chapel. The Music of the Cubes, Diversions Books, 2006. Critical comments on this subject: 'Rosslyn Chapel – Music of the Cubes' (or should that be 'Rubes'?), in: The BS Historian. Sceptical Commentary on Pseudohystory and the Paranormal, February 2008, in http://bshistorian.wordpress.com/2007/05/28/rosslyn-chapel-music-of-the-rubes/(January 12, 2011).

What began as a means for singing students to improve their voice training with the aid of the visual biofeedback, today continues to be used in other fields – such as in attractor reconstructions of the voice as they were conducted by Hans H. Diebner and Sebastian Fischer at ZKM (Centre for Art and Media Technology in Karsruhe, Germany) in 2001 (fig. 3a-b/p. 202, 203). By varying the voice, different patterns (attractor patterns) are obtained in a purely digital phase-space representation. In the *Club Moss Field Generator*, Maurmair managed to link the analogue and electronic domain with the aid of a microphone and loudspeaker that were connected to it as a frequency generator. In order to amplify the effect, he placed microscopic club moss spores on the membrane, which, depending on the pitch, form a characteristic pattern because the membrane vibrates at different intensities at different spots.[3] The same setting can be used to highlight different aspects according to the present focus of interest – and, of course, the shift of focus changes the significance of the grains used: They can be seen as tracer material for the vibrations caused by the spoken sounds. Or the voices, or sounds, can trigger the pattern formations, in which case the focus is more on the biological material, which the visitor looks at in a magnified Petri dish in Maurmair's arrangement. Both cases are some kind of experimental arrangement, with one focussing on the acoustic aspect and the other on the (visual) reaction of the substrate. In the *Club Moss Field Generator*, the visitor can decide for himself whether he prefers to adopt his voice to the pattern by deliberately imitating a formation, or whether he wants to shape the pattern through his voice and aims to achieve a vibration variety in the visual result.

In his installations, Maurmair creates situations that contrast people's visual and auditory experiences in every-day life, presenting shifts such as unexpected chains of causation or a shift in weight of the two sensory modalities. The visitor not only experiences a discrepancy between the active and the passive process (blowing – being blown at), and the process of seeing and hearing but is also given the possibility of creating an acoustic formation via a visual reference and vice versa. Thus, the sensory offers provided by the artist to his audience uncurl only gradually and reveal astonishing versatility.

Figures

Fig. 1a-b: Edmond Couchot and Michel Bret: Pissenlit, 1990. Screenshots, interactive computer installation. From: Maria Zambrano: Grains in my pocket, 2005, in: http://belcikowski.org/la_dormeuse/images2/couchot_dandelion2-jpg (February 02, 2011). (p. 200)

Edmond Couchot, Michel Bret, 1998, in http://www-inrev.univ-paris8.fr/extras/Michel-Bret/cours/bret/travaux/presse/1998/BeauxArts_1998.htm (February 02, 2011).

Fig. 2: Ernst Florens Friedrich Chladni: Patterns of sound on round plate, 1787. (p. 201) From: Ernst Florens Friedrich Chladni: Discoveries about the Theory of Sound. With eleven copper plates, Weidmanns Erben und Reich: Leipzig 1787, Table 1.

Fig. 3a-b: Hans H. Diebner and Sebastian Fischer: LiveReo January 02, 2001. Screenshot and documentary photo of the interactive computer application. From: LifeReco, in: http://fisch-im-netz.gmxhome.de/livereco.html (February 02, 2011). (p. 202, 203)

---

3   At this point, I would like to mention that the tiny seeds of the lycopodium have made an astonishing career in various areas of Physics. Scottish botanist Robert Brown (1773–1858) experimented with the tiny sufficiently cohesive grains, which he suspended in water to observe the temperature-related motion of liquid particles. It was not before 1905 that Albert Einstein (1879–1955) and Marian von Smoluchowski (1872–1909) discovered the mathematical formula called Brownian motion of particles. In the late 19th century zoologist Friedrich Ahlborn (1858–1937) started to use the spores to photographically visualize and analyze the non-linear dynamics of turbulent flows.

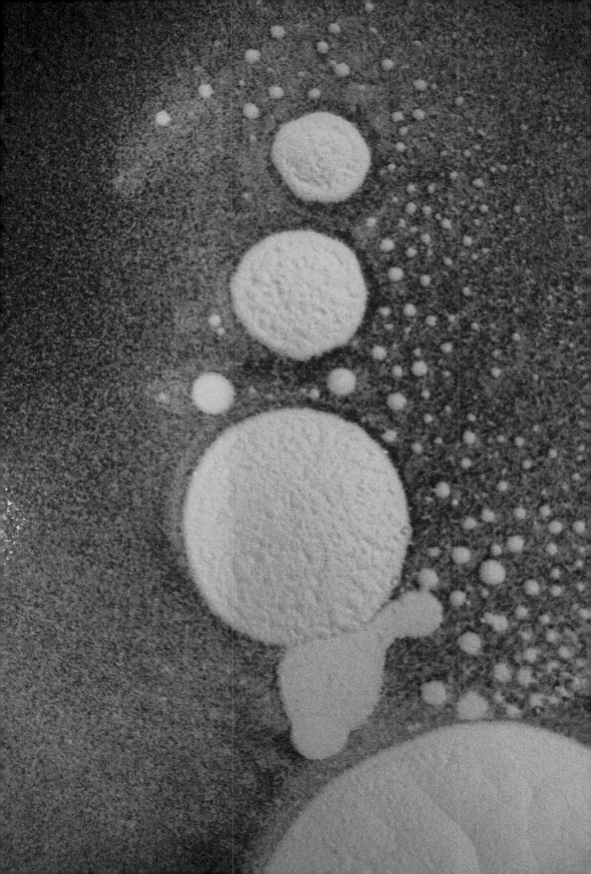

houseberge

Siebdruck, Zeichnung | screen print, drawing 2004

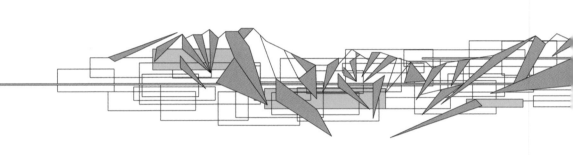

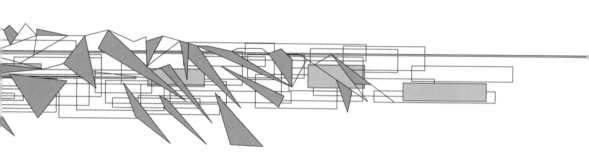

my home is my mountain

Siebdruck | screen print 2004, Briefmarke | stamp 2007

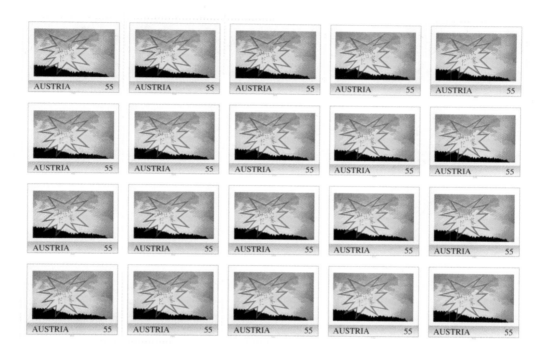

mons ex machina

mons ex machina

Artistische Wartungsarbeiten

Elsbeth Wallnöfer

„Die Geburt des Berges aus der Maschine" – dies zu veranschaulichen ist Ziel einer von Roland Maurmair konstruierten Maschine. Die aus dem Wechselspiel Natur – Kultur, Mensch – Natur erwachsenden Phänomene und deren Abfallprodukte (Sessellifte, Seilbahnen, Altöle etc.) werden gewissermaßen als „Urstoff", aus dem eine neue BergWelt entsteht, genutzt. Die Maschine wird mit zerkleinerten und pulverisierten Teilen von Seil- und Bergbahnen – zum Beispiel mit einem ausgedienten Zugseil der Stubaier Gletscherbahn – gefüttert. Dieses Material wird ebenso wie Altöle der Innsbrucker Nordkettenbahn als Mittel zur Herstellung großformatiger Graphiken herangezogen.

Die intensive, oft von kulturkritischen Argumenten geprägte, Auseinandersetzung mit der verschiedentlichen Nutzung der Alpen in den letzten Jahren erbittet geradezu eine Stellungnahme von Seiten der Kunst. Kahlschläge, aus welchen Gründen auch immer vorgenommen, der Eingriff mittels Technik, Architektur und Touristik in die Landschaft verweisen auf die Veränderung und das Prozesshafte der Alpen. Unabhängig von jeder moralischen Betrachtung wird der eigentliche Wandlungsprozess sichtbar, sobald man sein Augenmerk darauf lenkt. Ja, mehr noch. Es ist möglich, einen sonst möglicherweise zerstörerischen Ablauf umzukehren: Mit Hilfe zivilisatorischer Abfallprodukte kommt es zu einem konstruktiven Vorgang.

Aus dem von Natur und Kultur erodierten Berg entsteht ein neuer Berg. Und dieser wächst überhaupt erst durch den Rückgriff auf die ursprünglich zum Zweck des Eingriffs verwendeten Mittel. Der Berg, die alpine Landschaft entstehen aus dem Geiste der Maschine, dem Abfall der Maschine. *Mons ex machina* ist wie deus ex machina: die Geburt der Natur aus dem Geiste der Technik!

mons ex machina

artistic maintenance

Elsbeth Wallnöfer

„The mountain's birth from the machine" – a process that is visualized by a machine constructed by Roland Maurmair. The phenomena resulting from the interaction between nature and culture, mankind and nature, and the waste produced in this context (chair lifts, cable cars, waste oil, etc.) are used as the "source material" from which a new mountain world is created. The machine is fed with shredded and pulverized parts of cable cars and mountain railways – with an old disused hauling rope from the Stubai Glacier Railways. The material obtained in this way as well as waste oil from the Innsbruck Nordkette Railway are used to produce large-format graphics.

The intense debate, often characterized by culture-critical arguments, around the diverse use of the Alps over the past few years, has been calling for a statement from the arts community. Deforestation for all kinds of reasons, interference with nature via technology, architecture and tourism; all of this undermines the fact that the Alps are changing and undergoing a constant process of alteration. Regardless of any moral considerations, the actual process of change becomes visible when you focus on it. Even better. It is possible to reverse an otherwise potentially destructive process: With the aid of waste products created by modern civilization, a constructive process is initiated. The mountain eroded by nature and culture gives birth to a new one. And this mountain can only grow thanks to the products originally used to interfere with nature. The mountain – the Alpine scenery – is born from the mind of the machine, the waste produced by the machine.
Mons ex machina is like deus ex machina: nature is born from technology's mind!

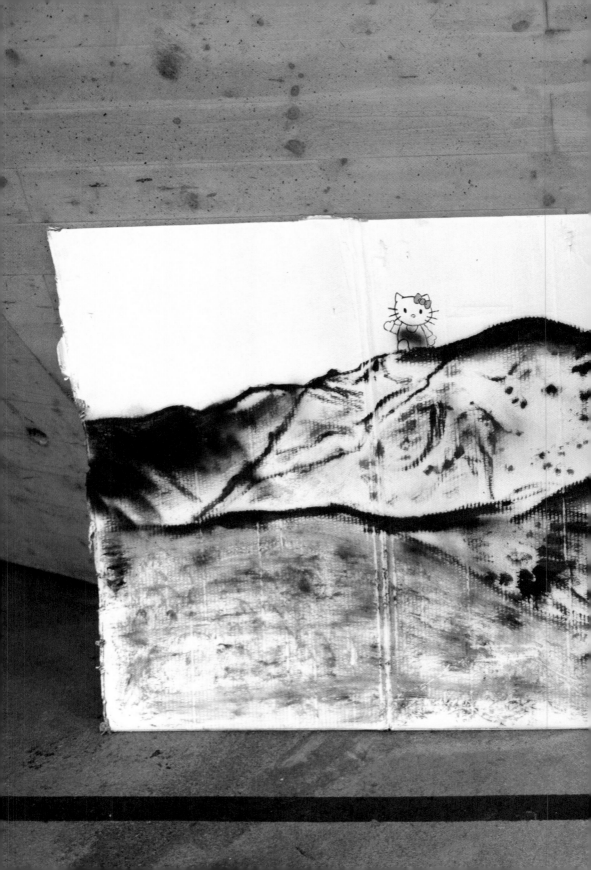

Biographie | Biography

Roland Maurmair

| *1975 | geboren in Innsbruck, Österreich, | | born in Innsbruck, Austria, |
| | lebt in Wien. | | lives in Vienna. |

2010	Artist in Residence, 12c – Raum für Kunst, Schnifis, Vorarlberg
2009	Promotion an der Universität für angewandte Kunst Wien,
	Institut für Kunst & Wissenstransfer
2008–09	Studium an der Universität für Bodenkultur Wien
2005–07	Leitung des Vereins medien.kunst.tirol
2005	Arthur Haidl Preis der Stadt Innsbruck
2005	Forschungsstipendium der Universität für angewandte Kunst Wien
2004	Artist in Residence, Paliano, Italien
2004	Diplom in Visuelle Mediengestaltung
2003–06	Artist in Residence, Künstlerhaus Büchsenhausen, Innsbruck
1998–99	Stipendium an der Gerrit Rietveld Academie, Amsterdam, Niederlande
1996–04	Universität für angewandte Kunst Wien, Visuelle Mediengestaltung
1996	Matura am BORG Innsbruck

Zahlreiche Einzelausstellungen und Beteiligungen im In- und Ausland. Unter anderem:
„Herde – Rudel – Schwarm", Ortner2, Wien | „Rabbitism", Eikon schAUfenster, quartier21, MQ Wien | „Dandelion", Swingr; Wien | „Landcruiser", Kunstraum Innsbruck | „Sculpturepark", UNO Fine Arts Gallery, New Orleans, USA | „Un space", MAK Gegenwartskunstdepot Gefechtsturm Arenbergpark, Wien | „Die Ordnung der Natur", OK Centrum, Linz | „Park of the Future", Amsterdam, Niederlande

2010	Artist in Residence, 12c – Raum für Kunst, Schnifis, Vorarlberg
2009	Doctor of Philosophy (PhD) – University for applied Arts Vienna,
	Centre for Art & Knowledge Transfer
2008–09	University of Natural Resources and Applied Life Sciences, Vienna
2005–07	Chairman of the association „medien.kunst.tirol"
2005	Arthur Haidl Price from the City of Innsbruck
2005	Research fellowship University for applied Arts Vienna
2004	Artist in Residence, Paliano, Italy
2004	Diploma Visual Media
2003–06	Artist in Residence, Künstlerhaus Büchsenhausen, Innsbruck
1998–99	Scholarship at the Gerrit Rietveld Academie, Amsterdam, the Nederlands
1996–04	University for applied Arts Vienna, Audiovisual Media Department
1996	Matura BORG Innsbruck

Numerous exhibitions and contributions in Austria and abroad:
„Herds – Packs – Flocks", Ortner2, Vienna | „Rabbitism", Eikon schAUfenster, quartier21, MQ Vienna | „Dandelion", Swingr, Vienna | „Landcruiser", Kunstraum Innsbruck | „Sculpturepark", UNO Fine Arts Gallery, New Orleans, USA | „Un space", MAK Contemporary Arts Centre at Gefechtsturm Arenbergpark, Vienna | „The Order of Nature", OK Center, Linz | „Park of the Future", Amsterdam, the Nederlands

S. | p.

Cover   *f*ck you, Birdy!* Photo | photograph 2006

1   *Schwärmen* Mischtechnik | *swarming* mixed technique, 70 x 50 cm, Vienna 2010

2–3   *untitled* Wandkratzerei | wall-scratching, 10 x 5 cm, Innsbruck 2006

4–5   *Nietzsche & Adorno* Zeichnung | drawing, 38 x 28 cm, Vienna 2009

6–7   *Ein Stück Almwiese#1* Siebdruck | *A piece of mountain pasture#1* screen print, 30 x 40 cm, Innsbruck 2008

8–9   *Invasion of the Cyber Crickets* Installation | installation, New Orleans 2007

10   *Ixodes ricinus* Objekt | object, 15 x 10 x 7 cm, Vienna 2011

13   *Morgen wird gestorben* Skizzenbucheintrag | *Let's die tomorrow* sketchbook entry, 21 x 14 cm, Innsbruck 2000

14–15   *Dandelion* Computergraphik | computer graphic, Vienna 2006

16   *Dandelion* Visualisierung | visualisation, Vienna 2006

17–21   *Dandelion* Klanginstallation, Ausstellungsansicht | sound installation, exhibition view, SWINGR – Raum für Kunst, Vienna 2006

22–23   *Landcruiser 1.3* interaktive Rauminstallation, Ausstellungsansicht | interactive multimedia installation, exhibition view, MAK Gefechtsturm, Vienna 2007

24   *Landcruiser 1.0* interaktive Rauminstallation, Ausstellungsansicht | interactive multimedia installation, exhibition view, Kunstraum Innsbruck 2003

25   *Landcruiser 1.0* interaktive Rauminstallation, Detailansicht | interactive multimedia installation, close-up view, Kunstraum Innsbruck 2003

26–27   *Flechten* Photo (aus Kryptogamen) | *Lichen* photograph (from Cryptogamia) 2004

28   *Algen.html* Siebdruck auf Nori-Algen | *Algae.html* screen print on Nori algae, 74 x 70 x 9 cm, OK Center, Linz 2005

29   *Algen.html* Siebdruck auf Nori-Algen | *Algae.html* screen print on Nori algae, 18 x 20 cm, Vienna 1998

30   *moos* Video Screenshots | *moss* video screenshots, 2005

31   *moos* Installation, Ausstellungsansicht | *moss* installation, exhibition view, Vienna 1998; OK Center, Linz 2005

32   *Farn* Installation, Ausstellungsansicht | *Fern* installation, exhibition view, OK Center, Linz 2005

33   *Farn* Video Screenshots | *Fern* video screenshots, 2004

34–35   *Bärlappfeldgenerator* interaktive Installation, Ausstellungsansicht | *Club Moss Field Generator* interactive installation, OK Center, Linz 2005

37   *index.html* Wandkratzerei | wall-scratching, 30 x 10 cm, Innsbruck 2005

39   *Schachtelhalm* (Equisetum) Mikroskopaufnahme | *horse tail* (equisetum) LM-micrograph, 2004

40–41   *Bios = Zoe* Steinkratzerei | stone-scratching, 20 x 16 x 6 cm, Innsbruck 2008

42–43   *and now something totally different* Photo | photograph, 2007

44   *go wild!* statische Versuchsanordnung | static experimental design, Vienna 1996

45   *go wild!* Detailansicht | close-up view, Vienna 1996

46   *Auslage in Arbeit* partizipatorische Installation, Andechsgalerie | *work in progress* participatory installation, Andechsgallery, Innsbruck 1999

47   *Auslage in Arbeit* Detailansicht | *window in progress* close-up view, Innsbruck 1999

48–49   *el viento viene, el hombre se va* intermediale Installation | intermedia installation, Amsterdam 1999

50–51   *Kluft reloaded* Lichtobjekt | *Cleft reloaded* light object, 100 x 20 x 21 cm, Vienna 2007

52   *Kastanienaktion* Intervention im öffentlichen Raum | *Chestnut action* intervention in public space, Innsbruck 2003

53   *Lassies letzter Augenblick* Installation | *Lassie's last moments* installation, Vienna 2005

54–55 *Mach das Licht aus, wenn Du gehst* Installation |
Turn off the lights when you leave installation, Vienna 2005; Innsbruck 2008

56–57 *Schmus'ma?* Kaltnadelradierung | *Wanna snog?* etching, 30 x 23 cm, Vienna 2009

58 *These hips are made for shaking* Video Screenshot | video screenshot, Vienna 2007

59 *These hips are made for shaking* Installation, Ausstellungsansicht, *Feine.Radikale* |
installation, exhibition view, *Fine.Radicals*, Freiraum quartier21, MQ, Vienna 2007

60 *These hips are made for shaking* Installation | installation, Vienna 2007

61 *These hips are made for shaking* Video Screenshots | video screenshots, Vienna 2007

62 *Blinde Kuh* Zeichnung | *Blind man's buff* drawing, 21 x 16 cm, Innsbruck 2005

63 *Blinde Kuh* Performance | *Blind man's buff* performance, Sandesalm 2008

64–67 *Punkcorn* Lichtinstallation | light installation, Galerie 39 Dada, Vienna 2008

68 *Porno* Radierung | etching, 27 x 22 cm, Vienna 2008

69 *Porno* Installation | installation, Galerie 39 Dada, Vienna 2008

70–71 *Gefahrenquelle* Intervention | *Source of Danger* intervention, *performIC* Innsbruck 2011

73–77 *If you have to be a monkey, be a Gorilla* Objekte (Beton) | objects (concrete),
New Orleans 2007; Innsbruck 2008

78 *Schau nit so, sonst bleibt's dir no!* Siebdruck (Serie Tierversuche) | *Don't give me that look -
it might not go away!* screen print (Bioassays series), 32 x 24 cm, Vienna 2006

79 *Ich bin doch keine Mouse!* Siebdruck (Serie Tierversuche) |
I am not a mouse! screen print (Bioassays series), 32 x 24 cm, Vienna 2007

80 *First I liked Vietnam, now I love Germany* Siebdruck (Serie Tierversuche) |
screen print (Bioassays series), 32 x 24 cm, Vienna 2007

81 *Mu* Siebdruck | screen print, 28 x 21 cm, Innsbruck 2005

82–83 *Kill Pandas* Zeichnung | drawing, 29 x 21 cm, Vienna 2008

84 *UN-Soldat gibt Tarnung auf* Siebdruck, coloriert |
UN soldier uncovered screen print, colored, 29 x 21 cm, Innsbruck 2007

85 *agent lemon* Objekt | object, Innsbruck 2004

86–97 *Serie Attacke* C-Prints auf LKW Plane | *Attack series* c-prints on lorry canvas

86–87 *Attacke!* C-Print (Tischdecke) | *Attack!* c-print (table cloth), 100 x 100 cm, Innsbruck 2004

88–89 *Blind ones see more* C-Print | c-print, 67 x 50 cm, Innsbruck 2004

90–91 *Attacke!* C-Print | *Attack!* c-print, 200 x 140 cm, Café Corso – Herbert Fuchs Räume,
Innsbruck 2004

92–93 *Yo!* C-Print | c-print, 67 x 50 cm, Innsbruck 2004

94–95 *Behind enemy lines* C-Print | c-print, 67 x 50 cm, Innsbruck 2004

96–97 *Neulich in Ramallah* C-Print | *Lately in Ramallah* c-print, 67 x 50 cm, Innsbruck 2004

98 *Die Afrikaner kommen* Siebdruck | *The Africans are coming!* screen print,
58 x 42 cm, Innsbruck 2005

99–101 *Die Afrikaner kommen!* Sticker, 12 x 5 cm, Innsbruck, Barcelona, Vienna, Munich 2005

102–103 *Die Afrikaner kommen!* Siebdruck |
The Africans are coming! screen print, 75 x 50 cm, Innsbruck 2005

104–105 *Die Afrikaner kommen!* Sticker, Innsbruck, Barcelona, Vienna, Munich 2005

107 *Separatistenkongress* Installation | *Separatists' Congress* installation,
Galerie Area 53, Vienna 2008

108–111 *The great escape* Objekt | object, Galerie Area 53, Vienna 2008

113 *Ein Stück Almwiese#2* Siebdruck | *A piece of mountain pasture#2*, screen print,
28 x 21 cm, Innsbruck 2008

114–115 *Sind wir nicht alle ein bisschen endo?* Klanginstallation | *Aren't we all a little bit endo?*
sound installation, Vienna 2000

116–117 *Rabbitism* Ausstellungsansicht | exhibition view, Innsbruck 2008

118, 123 *Rabbitism* Photo | photograph, Kunstraum Innsbruck 2007

119 *Psycho Rabbit* Zeichnung | drawing, 29 x 21 cm, Innsbruck 2006

120   *His Master's Voice* Siebdruck | screen print, 28 x 21 cm, Innsbruck 2009

121, 125 *Rabbitism* Video Screenshots | video screenshots, Vienna 2007

126–127 *Rabbitism* Kaltnadelradierung | etching, 22 x 18 cm, Vienna 2007

129   *accident#1 – Lügen haben kurze Beine* Objekt | *Lies have short legs* object, Vienna 2009

130   *Die Meistgesuchten (Serie Helden der Kindheit)* Siebdruck | *Most Wanted (Childhood Heroes series)* screen print, 70 x 50 cm, Vienna 2009

131   *USB Duck* Objekt | object, (1/5), 10 x 6 x 5 cm, Galerie Stalzer, Vienna 2009

133   *accident#2 – Raupe* Objekt | *Caterpillar* object, (1/5), 33 x 7 x 5 cm, Vienna 2009

134–135 *Invasion of the Cyber Crickets VS.1* primitive Medieninstallation | primitive media installation, UNO Center, New Orleans 2007

136–137 *Invasion of the Cyber Crickets VS.3,* Galerie Stalzer, Vienna 2009

138   *Invasion of the Cyber Crickets VS.2* unten | below, Innsbruck 2008

139   *Invasion of the Cyber Crickets VS.1* auch: 138 oben | see also: 138 above, New Orleans 2007

140–141 *Nest* Installation, Detail | installation detail, Kaufhaus Tyrol, Innsbruck 2006

143   *Nest* Installation, Ausstellungsansicht | installation, exhibition view, Innsbruck 2006

144   *Natural amplifier* Kaltnadelradierung | etching, 32 x 23 cm, Vienna 2007

145   *untitled* Mischtechnik | mixed technique, Innsbruck 2006

147   *Wenn Du glaubst, es geht nicht mehr, kommt irgendwo ein Lichtlein her (Serie Helden der Kindheit)* Siebdruck | *When you think there is no way forward a light will suddenly turn on somewhere (Childhood Heroes series)* screen print, 60 x 40 cm, Vienna 2009

148–149 *Blind Date III* Siebdruck, coloriert | screen print, colored, 28 x 21 cm, Vienna 2006

150–151 *Die Afrikaner kommen!* Stickers | *The Africans are coming!* stickers, 2005

151   *Ich Jane, du Tarzan* Stencil, Mischtechnik | *Me Jane, You Tarzan* stencil, mixed technique, 70 x 50 cm, Vienna 2008

152   *Blind Date II* Siebdruck, coloriert | screen print, colored, 28 x 21 cm, Innsbruck 2005

153   *Wenn ich groß bin, werde ich Bildungsbudget (Serie Helden der Kindheit)* Siebdruck | *When I'm older I wanna be an education budget (Childhood Heroes series)* screen print, 58 x 42 cm, Innsbruck 2010

154   *Bienvenido negrito!* Siebdruck coloriert | screen print, colored, 30 x 40 cm, Innsbruck 2006

155   *These things happen, when you're dreaming (Serie Helden der Kindheit)* Siebdruck | *(Childhood Heroes series)* screen print, 40 x 62 cm, Innsbruck 2010

156–157 *Free your ass, your mind will follow (Serie Helden der Kindheit)* Siebdruck | *(Childhood Heroes series)* screen print, 76 x 54 cm, Vienna 2009

158   *Mein Kaffee* Composing | *my coffee* composing, Vienna 2000

159   *170 braun keine* Reisepass Kopie | passport copy Roland Maurmair

160   *Hannibals Zug über die Alpen* Happening | *Hannibal's crossing of the Alps* happening, Brussels 2000

161   *Doppelspion mit Tarnkappe* Intervention | *Double agent with a magic hat* intervention, Innsbruck 1999

162   *Monochromalheur* Siebdruck | screen print, 60 x 40 cm, Innsbruck 2004

163   *Am Grab von Kasimir M.* Objekt | *At Kasimir M.'s grave* object, 10 x 10 cm, Amsterdam 1999

164–165 *Sumsizäpfchen* Objekt | *Sumsi suppositories* object, 11 x 7 x 2 cm, Innsbruck 2000

166   *Fuck, it's raining!* Siebdruck, coloriert | screen print, colored, (28 x 21 cm) Innsbruck 2005

167   *Raindrums* Installation | installation, Park of the Future, Amsterdam 2000

168   *Saigon ultra* Objekt | object, 20 x 14 x 5 cm, Vienna 2001

169   *The Never Miss a Mango-Tour* Composings, Vietnam; Austria 2004

170   *Burqababe* Objekt | object, Vienna 2010

171   *Burqababe, shopping* Zeichnung | drawing, 29 x 21 cm, Vienna 2009

172   *Transparenz des Bösen oder Maya und ihre Freunde halb zu Gast bei der halben Familie Gott* Mischtechnik | *Transparency of the evil or Half of Maya and her friends visiting half the God family* mixed technique, 140 x 50 cm, Innsbruck 2005

173   *Schlechter Empfang* Photo | *bad reception* photograph, Stadtturmgalerie Innsbruck 2004

174   *Camel²* Objekt | object, 10 x 9 x 3 cm, Innsbruck 1996

175   *Bluesbrüder* C-Print | c-print, 42 x 29 cm, Vienna 1998

176   *12 Monkeys* Siebdruck, coloriert | screen print, colored, 33 x 33 cm, Innsbruck 2006

177   *Jesus fue un terrorista* Siebdruck | screen print, 42 x 29 cm, Innsbruck 2007

178–179 *The legendary Piepshow* Multiple, Innsbruck 2004

180–181 *Nachtvogel* Zeichnung | *Night owl (tu-whit tu-whoo)* drawing, 29 x 21 cm, Vienna 2009

182   *Manticor* Objekt | object, 12c – Raum für Kunst, Schnifis 2010

183   *Ich wollt, ich wär ein Maulwurf* Objekt | *I wanna be a mole* object, 12c – Raum für Kunst, Schnifis 2010

184–185 *Manticor* Mischtechnik | mixed technique, 32 x 24 cm, Vienna 2009

186–187 *untitled* Kartoffeldruck | potatoe print, 70 x 50 cm, Vienna 2010

189   *Bumblebee Kavallerie* primitives Medienobjekt | *Bumblebee Cavalry* primitive media object, Ortner2, Vienna 2010

190–191 *Dosenthunfisch Schwarm* Installation (50 Stück) | *School of canned tuna* installation (edition of 50), Ortner2, Vienna 2010

192–193 *untitled* Kartoffeldruck | potatoe print, Vienna 2010

194–195 *Konvoi* Kaltnadelradierung | *Convoy* etching, 29 x 19 cm, Vienna 2010

197   *Sind wir nicht alle ein bisschen endo?* Installationsansicht | *Aren't we all a little bit endo?* installation view, Vienna 2000

199   *heavy-G-rain* Installationsansicht | installation view, White Club Space#4, Salzburg 2009

201–202 *Bärlappfeldgenerator* interaktive Installation, Ausstellungsansicht | *Club Moss Field Generator* interactive installation, OK Center, Linz 2005

205   *heavy-G-rain* Installationsansicht | installation view, Salzburg 2009

206   oben: *Separatistenkongress* Detail | above: *Separatists' Congress* detail, Vienna 2008

206   unten: *Dandelion* | below: *Dandelion*, Vienna 2006

207   *Bärlappfeldgenerator* | *Club Moss Field Generator*, OK Center, Linz 2005

209   *Bärlappfeldgenerator* Installationsdetail | *Club Moss Field Generator* installation detail, OK Center, Linz 2005

210   *Nockspitze* (Serie houseberge) Siebdruck | (houseberge series) screen print, 65 x 50 cm, Innsbruck 2005

211   *fad (Serles)* Zeichnung | *boring (Serles)* drawing, 21 x 15 cm, Innsbruck 2005

212–213 *Nordkette* (Serie houseberge) Siebdruck | (houseberge series) screen print, 65 x 50 cm, Innsbruck 2005

214   *my home is my mountain* Siebdruck | screen print, 90 x 60 cm, Innsbruck 2004

215   *my home is my mountain* Briefmarken | stamps, Innsbruck 2007

216–217 *mons ex machina* Installationsdetail | installation detail, kooio, Innsbruck 2010

218–219 *mons ex machina* Intervention, Innsbruck Hafelekar 2010

220–221 *mons ex machina* Intervention, Ausstellungsansicht | intervention, exhibition view, kooio, Innsbruck 2010

222   *Kailash (mons ex machina)* Mischtechnik | mixed technique, Nordkettenbahnen 210 x 105 cm, Innsbruck 2010

223   *MM I- MM III* Objekte | objects, 12 x 8 cm, kooio, Innsbruck 2010

224–225 *Parnass (mons ex machina)* Mischtechnik | mixed technique, 210 x 105 cm, Nordkettenbahnen Innsbruck 2010

226–227 *Nordkette (mons ex machina)* Mischtechnik | mixed technique, 240 x 40 cm, Nordkettenbahnen Innsbruck 2010

229   *12ender* Objekt | object, 12 x 7 x 18 cm, Vienna 2011

234   *Nature's Revenge* C-Print | c-print, 70 x 50 cm, Vienna 2006

236–237 *Wer das liest, ist ein Bleichgesicht* Kaltnadelradierung | *Read this, paleface!* etching, 19 x 14 cm, Vienna 2010

238–239 *Landebahn* Raumzeichnung | *runway* room drawing, 60 x 30 cm, 12c – Raum für Kunst, Schnifis 2010

240–241 *Blinde Kuh* Performance | *Blind man's buff* performance, Sandesalm 2008

Impressum | Colophon

Nature's Revenge | insight · concrete · jungle

Herausgegeben von | Edited by: Roland Maurmair

Mit Beiträgen von | Contributions by: Manfred Faßler, Thomas Feuerstein, Inge Hinterwaltner, Tereza Kotyk, Otto E. Rössler, Bernhard Tilg und Elsbeth Wallnöfer.

Lektorat | Proofreading: Konstantin Teske, Petra Möderle
Übersetzung | Translation: Heidelinde Holz
Graphik | Design: Roland Maurmair
Satz und Druckvorbereitung | Layout: Tommi Bergmann, Roland Maurmair
Photographie | Photographs:
falls nicht anders angegeben | unless otherwise indicated: Roland Maurmair
Thomas Böhm S. | p. 223 • Markus Bstieler S. | p. 71 • Andreas Bucher S. | p. 62, 78–80, 94, 98, 99, 138, 139, 145, 162, 166, 176, 177, 210, 211, 214, 215 • Thomas Feuerstein S. | p. 24, 25 • Roland Icking S. | p. 18, 19, 20, 21 • Peter Kubelka S. | p. 0, 1, 4–7, 10, 50, 51, 56, 57, 68, 115, 116, 122, 123, 126, 136, 137, 144, 147–149, 151–155, 170, 171, 180, 181, 184–187, 189–195, 229, 236, 237 • Ralf Ohnmacht S. | p. 125, 127, 129, 132, 133 • Otto Saxinger S. | p. 28, 31, 32 • Jan Windszus S. | p. 114, 119
Druck | Print: REMAprint

Besonderen Dank an | Special thanks to: Mark Beckmann, Tommi Bergmann, Bianca Doninger, Franziska Heubacher, Heidi Holz, Petra Möderle, Konstantin Teske
und allen AutorInnen und Mitwirkenden | and to all authors and participants

Gefördert durch | Supported by:

ISBN 978-3-902833-19-8

Vertrieb Deutschland und Schweiz | Distribution Germany and Switzerland:
Vive Versa, Berlin
Vertrieb Europa und weltweit | Distribution Europe and worldwide:
JOHN RULE Art Book Distribution, London
Vertrieb USA und Kanada | Distribution USA and Canada:
Art Stock Books, IPG, Chicago

SCHLEBRÜGGE.EDITOR
quartier21 / MQ
Museumsplatz 1
1070 Wien
Austria
www.schlebruegge.com

www.maurmair.com

WER DA
IST
BLEICH

LIEST.

IN

ESICHT.

You think it's the end,
but it's just the beginning...

Bob Marley